MARTIN HENGEL

Crucifixion

In the ancient world and the folly of
the message of the cross

FORTRESS PRESS

PHILADELPHIA

Translated by John Bowden from the German *"Mors turpissima crucis*:
Die Kreuzigung in der antiken Welt und die 'Torheit' des 'Wortes vom
Kreuz"*, published in *Rechtfertigung. Festschrift für Ernst Käsemann zum
70. Geburtstag*, ed. J. Friedrich, W. Pöhlmann and P. Stuhlmacher, by
J. C. B. Mohr (Paul Siebeck), Tübingen, and Vandenhoeck and Ruprecht,
Göttingen, 1976, with substantial later additions by the author.

First American Edition by Fortress Press 1977

Translation © 1977 by SCM Press Ltd., London and
Fortress Press, Philadelphia

Library of Congress Cataloging in Publication Data

Hengel, Martin.
    Crucifixion in the ancient world and the folly of the
message of the cross.

    Translation of Mors turpissima crucis.
    Bibliography: p.
    Includes indexes.
    1. Crucifixion—History. 2. Jesus Christ—Crucifixion.
I. Title.
HV8569.H4613 1977   364.6'6   77-78629
ISBN 0-8006-1268-X

6449F77   Printed in the United States of America   1-1268

In Memory of
Elisabeth Käsemann
born 11 May 1947
died in the Argentine
24 May 1977

CONTENTS

ABBREVIATIONS

AAMz	Abhandlungen der Akademie der Wissenschaften, Mainz
AGJU	Arbeiten zur Geschichte des antiken Judentums und Urchristentums, Leiden
ANEP	*The Ancient Near East in Pictures*, ed. J. B. Pritchard, Princeton 1954
BGU	Ägyptische Urkunden aus den königlichen Museen zu Berlin: Griechische Urkunden I–VIII, 1895–1933
BJ	Josephus, *De Bello Judaico*
BZNW	Beihefte zur Zeitschrift für die Neutestamentliche Wissenschaft, Berlin
CAH	*The Cambridge Ancient History*
CC	Corpus Christianorum, Turnholt
CIL	Corpus Inscriptionum Latinarum, Berlin
DJDJ	Discoveries in the Judaean Desert of Jordan, Oxford 1955ff.
ET	English translation
EvTh	*Evangelische Theologie*, Munich
FGH	*Die Fragmente der Griechischen Historiker*, ed. F. Jacoby, Berlin 1923ff., reprinted Leiden 1957ff.
GCS	Die Griechischen Christlichen Schriftsteller der ersten 3 Jahrhunderte, Berlin
HTR	*The Harvard Theological Review*, Cambridge, Mass.
IEJ	*Israel Exploration Journal*, Jerusalem
JBL	*Journal of Biblical Literature*, Philadelphia
LCL	The Loeb Classical Library, London and New York
MBPF	Münchener Beiträge zur Papyrusforschung und antiken Rechtsgeschichte
MGWJ	*Monatsschrift für Geschichte und Wissenschaft des Judentums*, Breslau
MusHelv	*Museum Helveticum*, Basle

NF (NS)   Neue Folge (New Series)
NTS   *New Testament Studies,* Cambridge
PCZ   *Zenon Papyri,* ed. C. C. Edgar, Vols. I–IV; ed. O.
            Guéraud and P. Jouguet, Vol. V, Cairo 1925–40
PG   Patrologia Graeca, ed. J. P. Migne, Paris
PGM   *Papyri Graecae Magicae: Die griechischen Zauberpapyri*
            I–III, ed. K. Preisendanz, 2nd ed. Stuttgart 1973f.
POxy   *The Oxyrhynchus Papyri,* ed. B. P. Grenfell, A. S. Hunt
            et al., London 1898ff.
PTA   Papyrologische Texte und Abhandlungen, Bonn
PW   *Paulys Realencyclopädie der classischen Altertumswissen-*
            schaft (2. R. = second row, beginning with R), Stuttgart
RAC   *Reallexikon für Antike und Christentum,* Stuttgart
            1950ff.
RdQ   *Revue de Qumran,* Paris
RHDF   *Revue historique de droit français et étranger,* Paris
Roscher   W. H. Roscher, *Ausführliches Lexikon der griechischen*
            und römischen Mythologie, Leipzig 1884ff.
SAB   Sitzungsberichte der Deutschen (Preussischen) Aka-
            demie der Wissenschaften zu Berlin
SB   *Sammelbuch griechischer Urkunden aus Ägypten,* ed. F.
            Preisigke et al., Strassburg et al. 1915ff.
SBS   Stuttgarter Bibelstudien
SJ   Studia Judaica, Berlin
TBLNT   *Theologisches Begriffslexikon zum Neuen Testament,*
            Wuppertal 1967ff.
TDNT   *Theological Dictionary of the New Testament,* Grand
            Rapids, Michigan 1964ff.
ThB   Theologische Bücherei, Munich
ThLL   *Thesaurus Linguae Latinae,* Leipzig 1900ff.
ThViat   *Theologia Viatorum,* Berlin
WdF   Wege der Forschung, Darmstadt
WuD   *Wort und Dienst, Jahrbuch der theologischen Schule*
            Bethel, Bielefeld
WUNT   Wissenschaftliche Untersuchungen zum Neuen Testa-
            ment, Tübingen
ZTK   *Zeitschrift für Theologie und Kirche,* Tübingen

INTRODUCTION
Mors turpissima crucis

This study first appeared as an article in *Rechtfertigung. Festschrift für Ernst Käsemann zum 70. Geburtstag*, ed. J. Friedrich, W. Pöhlmann and P. Stuhlmacher, Tübingen and Göttingen 1976, 125–84, and the three Latin words of its original title, *mors turpissima crucis* ('the utterly vile death of the cross'), best sum up its content. They come from Origen, *Commentary on Matthew*, on 27.22ff. (Klostermann, GCS 38, p. 259): *non solum homicidam postulantes ad vitam, sed etiam iustum ad mortem et ad mortem turpissimam crucis* (asking not only life for a murderer but also death for an innocent man, indeed the utterly vile death of the cross). J. Schneider, *TDNT* VII, 573 n.15, gives these words as a quotation from Tacitus: he has evidently overlooked the dash which separates adjacent quotations from Tacitus and Origen in P. Winter, *On the Trial of Jesus*, SJ 1, 1961, 185 n.21. I am especially grateful to my assistant Helmut Kienle for clarifying this complicated state of affairs: he has given me untiring help in checking quotations, gathering scattered material and reading proofs. I am also grateful to Gottfried Schimanowski for his help, especially with the typescript. I am further deeply indebted to my colleague Professor Rengstorf of Münster for communicating the Josephus passages containing προσηλοῦν, σταυρός, σταυροῦν, and to the *Thesaurus Linguae Latinae*, Munich, for the occurrences of *patibulum*. The *Thesaurus* offers the richest material on the terms *crux, crucifigo*, etc. (IV, cols. 1220ff.), but the information in Stephanus, *Thesaurus Graecae Linguae* on ἀναρτάω, ἀνασκολοπίζω, ἀνασταυρόω, κρεμάννυμι, προσηλόω, σανίς, σταυρός and σταυρόω is very haphazard and needs to be supplemented by the concordances to the various individual Greek writers. An attempt has been made to include all available material in this study, but because of the shortness of the time available for it, a number of instances may have escaped my attention, especially as there are no adequate concordances for many writers. While the manuscript was at the printers my colleague H. Cancik made many valuable suggestions for improving and extending it and Professor Louis Robert of Paris sent important information by letter. The key works on the subject are listed in the bibliography; attention is called particularly to the works by Lipsius, Zestermann, Stockbauer, Fulda, Κεραμό-πουλλος, Blinzler, Dinkler and Peddinghaus, to the study by H.-W. Kuhn and to the unfortunately all too brief articles in *PW* by Hitzig and Latte. Mommsen's classic *Römisches Strafrecht* is still the most important work on the legal aspect of crucifixion. More recent studies on legal questions are often disappointing. In his monumental work *Die Quellen des Römischen Rechts*, Vienna 1953, L. Wenger does not even include the words 'Kreuz', 'Kreuzigung' in his extensive index; the same is true of later works on Roman penal law, e.g. W. Kunkel, *Kleine Schriften. Zum römischen Strafverfahren und zur römischen Verfassungsgeschichte*, 1974. P. Garnsey, *Social Status and Legal Privilege in the Roman Empire*, 1970, 126ff., gives a few instances. I am grateful to Dr W. Pöhlmann for calling my attention to this work and to a number of studies on the history of law. There is still an urgent need for a comprehensive study of crucifixion and capital law in antiquity, including the Jewish world.

The original German text has been revised and considerably enlarged for the English translation. I have tried not only to add new evidence but also to complete the interpretation of different texts. The whole work is meant to be a preparation for a more comprehensive '*theologia crucis*' of the New Testament.

Tübingen
January 1977

I

The 'Folly' of the Crucified Son of God

In I Corinthians 1.18 Paul says that in the eyes of 'those who are perishing', the 'word of the cross' is 'folly'. He goes on to emphasize the point further in v. 23 by saying that the crucified Christ is a 'stumbling-block' for the Jews and 'folly' for the Gentiles. The Greek word μωρία which he uses here does not denote either a purely intellectual defect nor a lack of transcendental wisdom. Something more is involved. Justin puts us on the right track when he describes the offence caused by the Christian message to the ancient world as madness (μανία), and sees the basis for this objection in Christian belief in the divine status of the crucified Jesus and his significance for salvation:

> They say that our *madness* consists in the fact that we put a *crucified man* in second place after the unchangeable and eternal God, the Creator of the world (*Apology* I, 13.4).

Justin later concedes that demons have caused stories to be told about miraculous powers of the 'sons of Zeus' and of their ascensions to heaven, 'but in no case . . . is there any imitation of the crucifixion' (55.1).[1] It is the crucifixion that distinguishes the new message from the mythologies of all other peoples.

---

[1] The remarks in 22.3f. are only apparently a contradiction of this: 'But if anyone objects (εἰ δὲ αἰτιάσαιτό τις) that he was crucified, this is in common with the sons of Zeus, as you call them, who suffered as we have now enumerated [in the previous chapter]. For according to the accounts, their sufferings and death were not all alike, but different. So his unique passion does not make him out to be inferior – indeed I will, as I have undertaken, show, as the argument proceeds, that he was superior.' These explicit apologetic remarks also make it clear that the dishonour involved

The 'folly' and 'madness' of the crucifixion can be illustrated from the earliest pagan judgment on Christians. The younger Pliny, who calls the new sect a form of *amentia* (*Epistulae* 10.96.4–8), had heard from apostate Christians that Christians sang hymns to their Lord 'as to a god' (*quasi deo*), and went on to examine two slave girls under torture. Of course the result was disappointing:

> I discovered nothing but a perverse and extravagant superstition.
>
> (*nihil aliud inveni quam superstitionem pravam immodicam.*)

It must have been particularly offensive for a Roman governor that the one who was honoured 'as a god' (*quasi deo carmen dicere*) had been nailed to the cross by the Roman authorities as a state criminal.[2] His friend Tacitus speaks no less harshly of a 'pernicious superstition' (*exitiabilis superstitio*) and knows of the shameful fate of the founder:

> Christus, from whom the name had its origin, suffered the extreme penalty during the reign of Tiberius at the hands of the procurator Pontius Pilate.
>
> (*auctor nominis eius Christus Tiberio imperitante per procuratorem Pontium Pilatum supplicio adfectus erat.*)

The 'evil' (*malum*) which he instigated spread all too quickly to Rome, 'where all things hideous and shameful from every part of the world meet and become popular' (*quo cuncta undique atrocia aut*

---

in the death of Jesus by crucifixion was one of the main objections against his being son of God. Justin attempts to counter this by pointing out that various sons of Zeus are said to have died in different ways and that therefore Jesus is not to be held in less esteem because of the special form of his death. Moreover, the decisive thing is not his death, but what he did: ὁ γὰρ κρείττων ἐκ τῶν πράξεων φαίνεται. Cf. also Justin, *Dialogue with Trypho* 8.3; 10.3; 90.1; 137.1ff. and M. Hengel, *The Son of God*, 1976, 91f.

[2] For Pliny and the Christians see especially R. Freudenberger, *Das Verhalten der römischen Behörden gegen die Christen im 2. Jahrhundert*, MBPF 52, ²1969, 189ff., on the term *superstitio*. Horace, *Satires* 2.3.79f. includes superstition among spiritual ailments:

quisquis luxuria tristive superstitione
aut alio mentis morbo calet . . .

(Anyone who is feverish with extravagance or gloomy superstition or some other mental disorder . . .)

pudenda confluunt celebranturque, Annals 15. 44.3). Tacitus' precise knowledge of Christians and his contempt for them are probably to be derived from the trials of Christians which he carried out when he was governor in the province of Asia.[3]

In his dialogue *Octavius*, Minucius Felix begins by putting on the lips of his pagan interlocutor Caecilius a pointed piece of anti-Christian polemic, part of which goes back to a work by the famous orator Cornelius Fronto, who lived at the time of Marcus Aurelius. According to Caecilius, Christians put forward 'sick delusions' (*figmenta male sanae opinionis*, 11.9), a 'senseless and crazy superstition' (*vana et demens superstitio*, 9.2) which leads to an 'old-womanly superstition' (*anilis superstitio*) or to the destruction of all true religion (*omnis religio destruatur*, 13.5). Not least among the monstrosities of their faith is the fact that they worship one who has been crucified:

> To say that their ceremonies centre on a man put to death for his crime and on the fatal wood of the cross (*hominem summo supplicio pro facinore punitum et crucis ligna feralia*) is to assign to these abandoned wretches sanctuaries which are appropriate to them (*congruentia perditis sceleratisque tribuit altaria*) and the kind of worship they deserve (9.4).

The Christian Octavius does not find it easy to shake off this last charge. His answer makes it clear that the death of Jesus on the cross was inevitably folly and scandal even for the early Christians. Their pagan opponents quite unjustly assert that Christians worship 'a criminal and his cross' (*hominem noxium et crucem eius*, 29.2). No criminal, indeed no earthly being whatsoever deserves to be regarded as a god. On the other hand, Octavius does not go any

---

[3] For Tacitus' account of the Christians see H. Fuchs, 'Der Bericht über die Christen in den Annalen des Tacitus', in V. Pöschl (ed.), *Tacitus*, WdF 97, 1969, 558–604; Freudenberger, op. cit., 180ff.; R. Syme, *Tacitus* II, Oxford 1958, 468f., 532f. See also the commentary by E. Koestermann, *Cornelius Tacitus Annalen* IV, 1968, 253ff. His theory that Nero did not persecute the Christians but 'Jewish supporters of the agitator Chrestus, named by Suetonius, *Claudius* 25.4, and wrongly identified by Tacitus with the Christians' (253) is quite untenable. In my view, the *supplicio adfectus* is an echo of the 'slaves' punishment' (*servile supplicium*), cf. Valerius Maximus 8.4.1; *Scriptores Historiae Augustae* 15.12.2 and Hadrian: *ut homicidam servum supplicium eum iure iubete adfici* (quotation according to E. Levy, *Gesammelte Schriften* II, 1969, 476).

further into the person of Jesus and his fate; instead he deals at
some length with the charge of worshipping the cross.

> Moreover, we do not reverence the cross, nor do we worship it. But
> you, who hold your wooden gods (*ligneos deos*) to be holy, also
> worship wooden crosses, as parts of your divine images. For what are
> the military emblems, the banners and standards in your camps, if
> not gilded and decorated crosses? Not only is the form of your signs
> of victory like the structure of the cross; it even recalls a man
> fastened to it (29.6f.).

Indeed, are they not aware that such a 'wooden god' might perhaps
have been part of a funeral pile or a gallows-tree (i.e. a cross: *rogi
. . . vel infelicis stipitis portio*, 24.6)? Octavius cannot deny the
shamefulness of the cross and therefore he is deliberately silent
about the death of Jesus. He seeks to ward off any attack by going
over to the counter-attack – making use of the argument that divine
effigies are contemptible, an argument which was already well tried
in Jewish apologetic: you are the ones who worship crosses and
divine effigies, which in some circumstances have a shameful origin.
He avoids the real problem, namely that the Son of God died a
criminal's death on the tree of shame. This was not appropriate for
a form of argument which was concerned to prove that the one God
of the Christians was identical with the God of the philosophers.
Octavius' evasion of the point indicates the dilemma which all too
easily led educated Christians into docetism.

Augustine has preserved for us an oracle of Apollo recorded by
Porphyry, given in answer to a man's question what he can do to
dissuade his wife from Christian belief. The god holds out little
hope:

> Let her continue as she pleases, persisting in her vain delusions, and
> lamenting in song a god who died in delusions, who was condemned
> by judges whose verdict was just, and executed in the prime of life
> by the worst of deaths, a death bound with iron.
>
> (*Pergat quo modo uult inanibus fallaciis perseuerans et lamentari
> fallaciis mortuum Deum cantans* [compare the wording in Pliny], *quem
> iudicibus recta sentientibus perditum pessima in speciosis ferro uincta mors
> interfecit, Civitas Dei* 19.23; p. 690 CC.)

This oracle, originally in Greek, admirably confirms the verdicts of

Pliny, Tacitus and Caecilius. The one whom Christians claim as their God is a 'dead God' – a contradiction in itself. And if that were not enough, he had been condemned justly, as a criminal, by his judges in the prime of life, i.e. before his time, to the worst form of death: he had to endure being fastened to the cross with iron nails.

All this evidence shows us the constantly varying forms of abhorrence at the new religious teaching. In comparison with the religious ideals of the ancient world the Christian message had inevitably to be described in Suetonius' words as a 'new and pernicious superstition' (*superstitio nova et malefica*, Nero 16.3). These accounts, with their marked contemptuous characterizations, are no coincidence. The heart of the Christian message, which Paul described as the 'word of the cross' (λόγος τοῦ σταυροῦ), ran counter not only to Roman political thinking, but to the whole ethos of religion in ancient times and in particular to the ideas of God held by educated people.[4]

True, the Hellenistic world was familiar with the death and apotheosis of some predominantly barbarian demigods and heroes of primeval times. Attis and Adonis were killed by a wild boar, Osiris was torn to pieces by Typhon-Seth and Dionysus-Zagreus[5] by the Titans. Heracles alone of the 'Greeks' voluntarily immolated himself on Mount Oeta.[6] However, not only did all this take

[4] Cf. the polemic of Celsus, Origen, *Contra Celsum* 3.55, against the 'wool-workers, cobblers and laundry workers', and 6.34, against Jesus himself.

[5] A. Henrichs, *Die Phoinikika des Lollianos*, PTA 14, 1972, 56–79, seeks traces of a mystery of Dionysus-Zagreus in the human sacrifice depicted in the fragment of a romance which he has edited for publication. However, the decisive point here seems to me to be that the sacrifice of a child, eating his heart and drinking his blood, coupled with an oath and other consequent excesses, are seen by the author and his readers as quite barbarous customs. Naive souls may have imagined that similar things went on at Christian services.

[6] Cf. M. Hengel, *The Son of God*, 1976, 25f., and on his death, Seneca, *Hercules Oetaeus*, 1725f.:

vocat ecce iam me genitor et pandit polos:
venio pater . . .

(See now my father calls me and opens the skies;
Father, I come . . .)

place in the darkest and most distant past, but it was narrated in questionable myths which had to be interpreted either euhemeristic-ally or at least allegorically [7] By contrast, to believe that the one pre-existent Son of the onė true God, the mediator at creation and the redeemer of the world, had appeared in very recent times in out-of-the-way Galilee[8] as a member of the obscure people of the Jews,[9] and even worse, had died the death of a common criminal on

---

He displays his *maiestas* in dying without any sign of pain (1745f.):

> *stupet omne vulgus, vix habent flammae fidem,*
> *tam placida frons est, tanta maiestas viro.*

(The whole crowd stands in speechless wonder, scarcely able to believe the flames, so calm the brow, so majestic the hero.)

The heavenly voice of the exalted Heracles speaks to Alcmene (1966ff.):

> ... *quidquid in nobis tui*
> *mortale fuerat, ignis evictus tulit:*
> *paterna caelo, pars data est flammis tua.*

(Whatever in me was mortal and of you has felt the flames and been vanquished: my father's part has been given to heaven, yours to the flames.)

While there may be some parallels between this portrayal of the apotheosis of the son of Zeus and the passion in the gospel of John, it is a far cry from the account in Mark (15.21, 34–36). Heracles' action was imitated by Pere-grinus Proteus, who set fire to himself at the Olympic Games of AD 165. See Lucian, *De morte Peregrini* 20–45, esp. 39: 'I leave the earth and go to Olympus'. My colleague Professor Cancik has pointed out that from its beginnings down to Roman times tragedy has contained the theme of the suffering of heroes (πάθη ἡρώων); cf. Herodotus 5.67, and H. Cancik, 'Seneca und die römische Tragödie', in *Neues Handbuch der Literatur-wissenschaft* III, ed. M. Fuhrmann, Frankfurt-am-Main 1974, 251–60. Of course the heroes of the Greek sagas are not gods who are immortal by nature, but men who by their actions have attained the status and vene-ration accorded to gods.

[7] See e.g. Plutarch, *De Iside et Osiride*, 22–78; cf. T. Hopfner, *Plutarch, über Isis und Osiris* II, Prague 1941 (reprinted Darmstadt 1967), 101ff. According to ch. 79 (382f.), Osiris is immaculate and free from any association with transitoriness and death.

[8] For 'Galilean' as a derogatory term used of zealots and Christians to the time of Julian, see M. Hengel, *Die Zeloten*, AGJU 1, Leiden-Köln ²1976, 57ff.; H. Karpp, 'Christennamen', *RAC* II (1114–1138) 1131.

[9] Celsus in Origen, *Contra Celsum* 4.36: 'the Jews who cower together in a corner of Palestine', cf. 6.78: 'And you, do you not believe that the son of God sent to the Jews is the most ridiculous makeshift of all?'

the cross, could only be regarded as a sign of madness. The real gods of Greece and Rome could be distinguished from mortal men by the very fact that they were *immortal* – they had absolutely nothing in common with the cross as a sign of shame (αἰσχύνη) (Hebrews 12.2),[10] the 'infamous stake' (*infamis stipes*),[11] the 'barren' (*infelix lignum*) or 'criminal wood' (πανουργικὸν ξύλον),[12] the 'terrible cross' (*maxuma mala crux*) of the slaves in Plautus,[13] and thus of the one who, in the words of Celsus, was 'bound in the most ignominious fashion' and 'executed in a shameful way'.[14] Celsus

[10] I cannot share the view of H.-W. Kuhn (see bibliography), 1of., that Hebrews 12.2 is not influenced by the negative attitude towards crucifixion universal in antiquity, but primarily by the 'biblical Psalter'. The influence of the Psalter and the verdict of antiquity affect one another. For Hebrews 12.2 see now O. Hofius, *Der Christushymnus Philipper 2.6–11*, WUNT 17, 1976, 15ff.

[11] *Anthologia Latina* 415.23f.:

> *Noxius infami districtus stipite membra*
> *Sperat et a fixa posse redire cruce.*

(The criminal, outstretched on the infamous stake, hopes for escape from his place on the cross.)

Cf. also Lactantius, *Institutiones* 4.26.29: the question why God did not devise 'an honourable kind of death' (*honestum . . . mortis genus*) for Jesus, 'why by an infamous kind of punishment which may appear unworthy even of a man, if he is free, although guilty' (*cur infami genere supplicii, quod etiam homine libero quamuis nocente uideatur indignum*). Arnobius, *Adversus nationes* 1.36, makes similar remarks.

[12] Seneca, *Epistulae morales* 101.14; cf. Minucius Felix, *Octavius* 24.6: *deus enim ligneus, rogi fortasse vel infelicis stipitis portio, suspenditur, caeditur. . . .* Behind this is probably to be found the old Roman conception of the *arbor infelix*, consecrated to the gods of the underworld, as a means of execution, see below p. 39. For the 'criminal wood' see the London magical papyrus *PGM* V, 73 (Preisendanz/Henrichs I, p. 184).

[13] See the numerous instances in *ThLL* IV, 1259: *Captivi* 469; *Casina* 611; *Menaechmi* 66, 849 (*abscedat in malam magnam crucem*); *Poenulus* 347 (*i directe in maxumam malam crucem*); *Persa* 352; *Rudens* 518; *Trinummus* 598. The simple *mala crux* is even more frequent. Thus above all in Plautus, but see also Ennius, *Annals* 11, fr. 4 (Argenio, p. 114, lines 349f.): *malo (sic) cruce, fatur, uti des, Iuppiter.* Even more vividly in C. Sempronius Gracchus: *Eo exemplo instituto dignus fuit, qui malo cruce periret* (quoted by Sextus Pompeius Festus, *De Significatu Verborum*, Mueller, p. 150; Lindsay, p. 136).

[14] Origen, *Contra Celsum* 6.10: πίστευσον ὃν εἰσηγοῦμαί σοι τοῦτον εἶναι υἱὸν θεοῦ, κἂν ᾖ δεδεμένος ἀτιμότατα ἢ κεκολασμένος αἴσχιστα, cf. 2.9.68. Achilles Tatius, 2.37.3, calls Ganymede, who was snatched away by an eagle and

8 *Crucifixion*

puts these phrases in the mouths of Christians as a parody of the faith which they require: they are very similar to the carefully calculated exuberance in Cicero's documentary 'speech' against Verres (it was never delivered), in which the orator makes the charge that the former governor of Sicily inflicted the *crudelissimum taeterrimumque supplicium*[15] on a Roman citizen with the utmost haste and without further investigation, having it carried out immediately.

Some further Greek and Latin evidence may serve to show that this statement by the great statesman and legal advocate, like other similar ones, was something more than an isolated 'aesthetic judgment'[16] – as has been suggested recently – remote from the views of ordinary people and the rest of the ancient world. For example Josephus, who as Jewish adviser to Titus during the siege of Jerusalem was witness to quite enough object lessons of this kind, describes crucifixion tersely and precisely as 'the most wretched of deaths' (θανάτων τὸν οἴκτιστον). In this context he reports that a threat by the Roman besiegers to crucify a Jewish prisoner caused the garrison of Machaerus to surrender in exchange for safe conduct.[17] According to Lucian, the letter T was given its 'evil significance' by the 'evil instrument', shaped in the form of a *tau*, which tyrants erected to 'hang men on': 'I think we can only punish Tau by making a T of him.'[18] In the treatise on dreams by Artemidorus, to

---

was like a crucified figure (καὶ ἔοικεν ἐσταυρωμένῳ, conj. Jacobs), a θέαμα . . . αἴσχιστον, μειράκιον ἐξ ὀνύχων κρεμάμενον. In Origen, *Contra Celsum* 6.34 (cf. 36, end), Celsus combines in a contemptuous way the nailing of Jesus to the cross with his lowly trade as a carpenter and mocks Christian talk of the 'tree of life' and the 'resurrection of the flesh through the wood (of the cross)': 'What drunken old woman, telling stories to lull a small child to sleep, would not be ashamed of muttering such preposterous things?' Cf. Minucius Felix, above, p. 3.

[15] 2.5.165: *apud te nomen civitatis ne tantum quidem valuisse ut dubitationem aliquam (crucis), ut crudelissimi taeterrimique supplicii aliquam parvam moram saltem posset adferre.* (That this mention of his citizenship had not even so much effect on you as to produce a little hesitation or to delay even for a little the infliction of that most cruel and disgusting penalty.)

[16] Thus H.-W. Kuhn (see bibliography), 8.

[17] *BJ* 7.202ff. (the quotation comes from 203); cf. Lucian, *Prometheus* 4. He calls the crucified Prometheus (see pp. 11f. below) an οἴκτιστον θέαμα πᾶσι Σκύθαις.

[18] *Iudicium vocalium* 12: τῷ γὰρ τούτου (viz. the 'Tau') σώματί φασι τοὺς

dream that one is flying among the birds can only be of ill omen for criminals, 'for it brings the death penalty to criminals, and very often through crucifixion'.[19] Similarly, in his didactic astrological poem, Pseudo-Manetho enumerates the criminals who must justifiably expect crucifixion, and includes among them murderers, robbers, mischief-makers (ἐμπεδολώβας) and deceivers:

Punished with limbs outstretched, they see the stake as their fate; they are fastened (and) nailed to it in the most bitter torment, evil food for birds of prey and grim pickings for dogs.

(στρεβλὰ κολαζόμενοι σκολοπηΐδα μοῖραν ὁρῶσιν
πικροτάτοις κέντροισι προσαρτηθέντες ἐν ἥλοις,
οἰωνῶν κακὰ δεῖπνα, κυνῶν δ' ἑλκύσματα δεινά.)[20]

This evidence from the third century AD shows how widespread was the death penalty and the use of crucifixion even in the later empire; nor had there been any change in the negative attitudes towards crucifixion. From the time of Plautus, that is, from the third century BC onwards, there is evidence of the use of *crux* as a vulgar taunt among the lower classes. It can be found on the lips of slaves and prostitutes,[21] and is comparable with *furcifer*, *cruciarius*

τυράννους ἀκολουθήσαντας καὶ μιμησαμένους αὐτοῦ τὸ πλάσμα ἔπειτα σχήματι τοιούτῳ ξύλα τεκτήναντας ἀνθρώπους ἀνασκολοπίζειν ἐπ'αὐτά. ἀπὸ δὲ τούτου καὶ τῷ τεχνήματι τῷ πονηρῷ τὴν πονηρὰν ἐπωνυμίαν συνελθεῖν. ('For they say that their tyrants, following his figure and imitating his build, have fashioned timbers in the same shape and crucify men upon them; and that it is from him that the sorry device gets its sorry name.')

[19] *Oneirocriticon* 2.68 (Pack, p. 192): πανούργοις δὲ πονηρόν. τοὺς γὰρ ἀλιτηρίους κολάζει, πολλάκις δὲ καὶ διὰ σταυροῦ; cf. 2.56 (p. 185): κακούργῳ μὲν ἰδόντι σταυρὸν βαστάσαι σημαίνει, similarly 1.76 (p.82); Plutarch, *Moralia* 554 A/B (see p. 77 below): *Anthologia Graeca* 9.378 (Beckby, III, p. 234) and 9.230 (III, p.658).

[20] *Apotelesmatica* 4.198ff. (Koechly, p.69). Prof. Cancik conjectures ἔνηλοι for the difficult ἐν ἥλοις. The adjective ἔνηλος is attested by the old glossaries with the meaning 'nailed', see Liddell and Scott, 9th ed., 1940, s.v. Cf. 1.148f. (p.90): ἄλλον δ'ἀκλειῶς μετέωρον ἀνεσταυρώσας, οὗ τέτατ' ἀνδροφόνοις περὶ δούρασιν ἡλοπαγὴς χείρ, similarly 5.219ff. (p. 108). On this see F. Cumont, *L'Égypte des astrologues*, Brussels 1937, 197 n.1.

[21] See *ThLL* IV, 1259; Plautus, *Aularia* 522; *Bacchides* 584; *Casina* 416 (conj. Camerarius); *Persa* 795; Terence, *Eunuch* 383; Petronius, *Satyricon* 126.9; cf. 58.2: *crucis offla* (=*offula*), *corvorum cibaria*, 'gallows-bird', 'carrion'.

or even *patibulatus*:[22] an English equivalent might be 'gallows-bird', 'hang-dog'. The abusive *i in malam maximam crucem* thus meant something like 'Be hanged!'[23] Varro, Cicero's contemporary, uses the offensive word *crux* as a vivid illustration for his etymological theory: *lene est auribus cum dicimus 'voluptas', asperum cum dicimus 'crux'* ... *ipsius verbi asperitas cum doloris quem crux efficit asperitate concordet* (to say 'pleasure' is gentle on the ears, but to say 'cross' is harsh. The harshness of the latter word matches the pain brought on by the cross).[24] The learned man presupposes that everyone will accept this argument. We may no doubt assume that this horrible word did not sound any better in the ears of a slave or foreigner (*peregrinus*) than it did to a member of the Roman nobility.

Even Paul's Greek audience could hardly have approved of the λόγος τοῦ σταυροῦ, much less the Jews who could see the Roman crosses erected in Palestine, especially when they could hardly forget the saying about the curse laid upon anyone hanged on a tree (Deut. 21.23). A crucified messiah, son of God or God must have seemed a contradiction in terms to anyone, Jew, Greek, Roman or barbarian, asked to believe such a claim, and it will certainly have been thought offensive and foolish.

[22] *Cruciarius*: *ThLL* IV, 1218: Seneca the Elder, *Controversiae* 7.6.2f., 6; Apuleius, *Metamorphoses* 10.7.5, etc.; cf. Isidore of Seville, *Etymologiae* 10.48f.: 'one worthy of the cross' (*cruciarius eo quod sit cruce dignus*). *Patibulatus*: Plautus, *Mostellaria* 53; cf. Apuleius, *Metamorphoses* 4.10.4.

[23] *ThLL* IV, 1258f.: Plautus, *Asinaria* 940; *Bacchides* 902; *Casina* 93, 641, 977; *Curculio* 611, 693; *Menaechmi* 915, 1017; *Mostellaria* 1133; *Poenulus* 271, 495, 511, 789, 1309 etc.; cf. p. 7 n. 13 above.

[24] *De lingua latina quae supersunt*, ed. Goetz/Schoell, p. 239. (I am grateful to Prof. Cancik for this comment.)

2

Prometheus and Dionysus: the 'Crucified' and the 'Crucifying' God

The only possibility of something like a 'crucified god' appearing on the periphery of the ancient world of the gods was in the form of a malicious parody, intended to mock the arbitrariness and wickedness of the father of the gods on Olympus, who had now become obsolete. This happens in the dialogue called *Prometheus*, written by Lucian, the Voltaire of antiquity. When describing how his hero is fastened to two rocks in the Caucasus, Lucian uses all the technical terms of a crucifixion: Prometheus is to be nailed to two rocks above a ravine in the sight of all, in such a way as to produce the effect of 'a most serviceable cross' (ἐπικαιρότατος . . . ὁ σταυρός).[1] Hermes and Hephaestus carry out their gruesome work like two slaves, threatened by their strict master with the same punishment if they weaken. The climax comes with the charge

---

[1] *Prometheus* 1: προσηλῶσθαι, . . . καὶ οὗτος ἅπασι περιφανὴς εἴη κρεμάμενος, . . . οὔτε γὰρ ταπεινὸν καὶ πρόσγειον ἐσταυρῶσθαι χρή . . . , . . . ὑπὲρ τῆς φάραγγος ἀνεσταυρώσθω ἐκπετασθεὶς τὼ χεῖρε . . . 2: . . . ἀντὶ σοῦ ἀνασκολοπισθῆναι αὐτίκα (nailed up . . . and he will be in full sight of everyone as he hangs there . . . We must not crucify him low and close to the ground . . . crucify him above the ravine with his hands stretched out . . . be crucified in your stead). For the model see Hesiod, *Theogony* 521f., and Aeschylus, *Prometheus* 52ff. Possibly Hesiod and Aeschylus already depicted the binding of Prometheus after the manner of an *apotympanismos*, see p. 70 below. Hesiod, *Theogony* 521, speaks of a post or pillar to which the god is fastened: δεσμοῖς ἀργαλέοισι μέσον διὰ κίον' ἐλάσσας (bound with inextricable bonds, driving a shaft through the middle). W. Marg, *Hesiod, Sämtliche Gedichte*, Zürich-Stuttgart 1970, 227f., conjectures 'a stake of shame (i.e. a pillory) . . . which was perhaps originally one of the pillars of heaven'. See Κεραμόπουλλος (see bibliography), 60–6; cf. also L. Gernet (see bibliography), 295f., 306 and 316; P. Ducrey (see bibliography), 210 n. 1 and the vases on plates I and II. Apollodorus 1.7.1 speaks of Prometheus being nailed.

made by Prometheus, the Titan, against Zeus: Prometheus is
ashamed that Zeus could be so petty and so vengeful as to 'deliver
so old a god to crucifixion' (ἀνασκολοπισθησόμενον πέμπειν
παλαιὸν οὕτω θεόν, ch. 7). It was necessary to make man in the
image of the gods, 'for I believed that the divinity was incomplete
without a counterpart and that only a comparison would show it to
be the happier being' (ch. 12). Moreover, worship of the gods and
sacrifice had been made possible only by the gift of fire: 'You have
crucified the author of the honour and the sacrifice offered to you!'
(ch. 17). Even Hermes, who is rarely at a loss for a word, cannot find
fault with these arguments of the γενναῖος σοφιστής; he tries to
console Prometheus by speaking of his gifts as a seer. Thus
reconciliation is achieved at the end. As a μάντις Prometheus
prophesies his own liberation by Heracles and his complete
rehabilitation – a crucified god can at best be tormented for a while;
he can never die.[2] It does not seem to me to be a coincidence that
the author of this biting parody in his *De morte Peregrini* mocks
Christians as 'poor devils' (κακοδαίμονες) 'who deny the Greek
gods and instead honour that crucified sophist and live according
to his laws'.[3]

A distinction should be made between the 'crucifixion' of the

[2] For the theme of the crucified Prometheus in connection with a parody
of the gods see also Lucian, *Iuppiter confutatus* 8 and *De sacrificiis* 6:
Prometheus was more than usually φιλάνθρωπος, καὶ τοῦτον εἰς τὴν Σκυθίαν
ἀγαγὼν ὁ Ζεὺς ἀνεσταύρωσεν (though well disposed to men, he was brought by
Zeus to Scythia [the barbarian land *par excellence*], where he was crucified);
Dialogi deorum 5 (1).1. There are also allusions to the crucifixion of Prometheus in Martial, *Liber spectaculorum* 7.1ff.; Ausonius, *Technopaegnion*
(*De historia*) 10.9ff. (Peiper, p. 163). One might also compare Andromeda,
who is freed by Perseus, see Manilius, *Astronomica* 5.551ff. (Housman, p.
71, see below, p. 77), and Aristophanes, *Thesmophoriazusae* 1011; also
Euripides, *Andromeda* frs. 122–8 (Nauck, pp. 397ff.); see also p. 70 below.
According to Philostratus, *Heroicus* 19.17 (Kayser II, p. 214). Heracles
crucifies the centaur Asbolus and writes 'this epitaph for him': 'I Asbolus,
who fear the punishment of neither men nor gods, hang on the pointed,
resinous fir, giving a great meal to the long-lived ravens.'

[3] *De morte Peregrini* 13: τὸν δὲ ἀνεσκολοπισμένον ἐκεῖνον σοφιστὴν αὐτὸν
προσκυνῶσιν καὶ κατὰ τοὺς ἐκείνου νόμους βιῶσιν. Cf. 11: ... ὃν ἔτι σέβουσι, τὸν ἄνθρωπον
τὸν ἐν τῇ Παλαιστίνῃ ἀνασκολοπισθέντα, ὅτι καινὴν ταύτην τελετὴν εἰσῆγεν ἐς (sic) τὸν
βίον (whom they still worship, the man crucified in Palestine, because he
introduced this new religion into life).

rebellious Titan Prometheus by Zeus, the father of the gods, and the report in Diodorus Siculus (3.65.5) about the crucifixion of the wicked *Lycurgus* by *Dionysus*. The two are quite different. Lucian's account is a bitterly angry mockery of the gods; Diodorus' account, on the other hand, is unique in ancient literature and derives from the genre of the historicizing, euhemeristic romance. According to E. Schwartz it goes back to the Alexandrian writer Dionysius Scytobrachion.[4] Lycurgus, king of Thrace, is said to have broken peace treaties with Dionysus, who had come from Asia as conqueror of the world. Thereupon Dionysus crossed the Hellespont and 'defeated the Thracian forces in battle. Lycurgus, whom he took prisoner, he blinded, tortured in every conceivable way and finally crucified' (καὶ τὸν Λυκοῦργον ζωγρήσαντα τυφλῶσαί τε καὶ πᾶσαν αἰκίαν εἰσενεγκάμενον ἀνασταυρῶσαι). This account has no religious connections; it is not even critical of religion, as is the case with Lucian. Rather, it is a realistic political representation of an idea which was particularly popular in Hellenistic times, that of Dionysus as conqueror of the world, which was adorned with the colours of the romance of Alexander. A cruel practice from the Persian and Macedonian wars underlies the motif of crucifixion. This was used as a punishment for rebellious vassals and usurpers. Plato was already familiar with it, and it had also been employed by Alexander and the Diadochi (see below, pp. 27ff., 73f.). The punishment of Lycurgus appears for the first time in Homer, who simply records that Zeus blinded the 'enemy of the gods' because of his wickedness towards the Maenads and the child Dionysus:

> The immortals, who live in blessedness, were angry with him, and Zeus the son of Cronos struck him blind. He did not live long after this, for he was hateful to all the immortal gods. No, I take no delight in fighting against the blessed gods (Diomede, in *Iliad* 6.138–41).

[4] See Drexler, 'Lykurgos', in: W. H. Roscher, *Ausführliches Lexikon der griechischen und römischen Mythologie* II, 2 (1897–99), 2194, and E. Schwartz, *De Dionysio Scytobrachione*, Diss. Bonn 1880, 46. Cf. Heracles and Asbolus (above, p. 12 n. 2).

The extraordinary paucity of the theme of crucifixion in the mythical tradition, even in the Hellenistic and Roman period, shows the deep aversion from this cruellest of all penalties in the literary world.

3

Docetism as a Way of Removing the 'Folly' of the Cross

With its paradoxical contrast between the divine nature of the pre-existent Son of God and his shameful death on the cross, the first Christian proclamation shattered all analogies and parallels to christology which could be produced in the world of the time, whether from polytheism or from monotheistic philosophy. We have points of comparison for the conceptions of exaltation, ascension and even resurrection. But the suffering of a god soon had to be shown to be mere simulation, rapidly followed by punishment for those humans who had been so wicked as to cause it: good examples of this are some stories about the god Dionysus: the fate of Lycurgus, which has already been mentioned, his fortunes among the pirates[1] or the account of his capture by Pentheus in the *Bacchae*.[2] Prometheus' words in Aeschylus, 'See what I, a god, suffer at the hands of gods' (ἴδεσθέ μ'οἷα πρὸς θεῶν πάσχω θεός, 93), are the exception which proves the rule. Thus the basic theme of christology, the humiliation and ignominious death of the pre-existent redeemer, presented in the first verse of the hymn in Philippians 2.6–11, is obscured, rather than elucidated, by reference

---

[1] *Homeric hymns* 7.12ff.: 'They attempted to bind him with crude bonds, but the bonds would not hold him and the withes fell far away from his hands and feet.' The hymn is a late one, from the Hellenistic period.

[2] Euripides, *Bacchae* 515ff.: the god must not suffer, and Pentheus will have to do penance for his arrogance in wanting to bind the god. Cf. 614ff.:

Dionysus: I delivered myself easily, and with no trouble.
Chorus: Did not Pentheus bind your hands with coils of chains?
Dionysus: It was here I scorned him; thinking that he fettered me he neither touched nor grasped me, but fed on fantasy.

to a pagan pre-Christian redeemer myth.[3] In particular, the gnostic 'docetism' which did away with the scandal of the death of Jesus on the cross in the interest of the impassibility of the God of the philosophers demonstrates that the gnostic systems are secondary attempts at an 'acute Hellenization' of the Christian creed, i.e. necessary consequences of a popular philosophical influence. On many occasions in the Graeco-Roman world we come across the idea that offensive happenings should not be ascribed to revered divine beings or demi-gods themselves, but only to their 'representations'. Thus Ixion, inflamed with love for Hera the spouse of Zeus, does not embrace the goddess herself but a cloud which has taken her shape – and as a punishment for his wickedness is bound to the wheel of the sun.[4] Helen, the daughter of Zeus and Leda, was really transported by Hermes to Egypt, where she remained safely until the conquest of Troy, whereas Paris possessed in 'empty delusion' (δοκεῖ μ'ἔχειν κενὴν δόκησιν, οὐκ ἔχων) her phantom (εἴδωλον), 'made out of heavenly ether' ((ὁμοιώσασ' ἐμοὶ εἴδωλον ἔμπνουν οὐρανοῦ ξυνθεῖσ' ἄπο) by Hera, who grudged Helen to Paris. This is what he took away to an adulterous union in Troy.[5] According to Ovid's *Fasti* (3.701ff.), the goddess Vesta carried off Caesar, her priest, to the heavenly halls of Jupiter immediately before his murder, and the assassins' weapon stabbed only his phantom:[6]

> *ipsa virum rapui simulacraque nuda reliqui;*
> *quae cecidit ferro Caesaris umbra fuit.*
> *ille quidem caelo positus Iovis atria vidit*
> *et tenet in magno templa dicata foro.*

[3] M. Hengel, *The Son of God*, 1976, 33ff.; on Phil. 2.6ff. see now O. Hofius, *Der Christushymnus Philipper 2.6–11*, WUNT 17, 1976.

[4] See Weizsäcker, Roscher II, 1, 766ff.; Waser, *PW* X, 2, 1373ff.

[5] Euripides, *Helena* 31ff.; cf. *Electra* 1283f.; also Bethe, *PW* VII, 2.2833ff. We can already find a man being transported by a god and being replaced by an εἴδωλον in Homer, *Iliad* 5, 311ff., 344ff., 445ff., 449ff., where Aeneas is rescued by his mother Aphrodite and Apollo. For Heracles see *Odyssey* 11.601ff.

[6] See E. Bickerman, 'Consecratio', in *Le culte des souverains dans l'Empire romain*, Entretiens sur l'antiquité classique 19, Vandoeuvres-Genève 1973, (1–25) 15f. The model for the transporting of Caesar seems to be that of his ancestor Aeneas.

(I myself carried the man away, and left nothing but his phantom behind. What fell by the sword was Caesar's shade. Transported to the sky he saw the halls of Jupiter and in the great Forum he has a temple dedicated to him.)

For Celsus or his Jewish authority, Jesus should have demonstrated his divinity by being transported either at the time of his capture or later, from the cross.[7]

The current trend in exegesis concerned with christology away from a one-sided orientation on the abysses of gnosticism towards a special concern with the Pauline theology of the cross is to be welcomed, because here we find ourselves confronted with the indispensable characteristic of Paul's preaching. Indeed, here we have the theological centre of the New Testament itself, which is grounded on the representative death of the messiah Jesus, a fact which cannot be dissolved into any kind of docetism, ancient or modern. It is important not to blur the sharp contours of Paul's remarks about the cross of Christ by including them in a questionable and hypothetical 'theology of the cross' which is supposed to extend to Justin, the gnostics of the second century AD and the apocryphal acts of the apostles.[8] The later interpretation of the

---

[7] Origen, *Contra Celsum* 2.68: εἰ δ'οὖν τό γε τοσοῦτον ὤφειλεν εἰς ἐπίδειξιν θεότητος, ἀπὸ τοῦ σκόλοπος γοῦν εὐθὺς ἀφανὴς γενέσθαι ('But if he was really so great he ought, in order to display his divinity, to have disappeared suddenly from the cross.') Cf. pp. 7f. n. 14 above.

[8] This danger is to be found in the account given by H.-W. Kuhn (see bibliography). After what I feel to be a questionable discussion of crucifixion in antiquity (3–11), he immediately continues with the role of the cross in Christian gnosticism (11ff.) and only comes to Paul at the end (27ff.). The great variety of speculative gnostic interpretations of the cross (see W. Foerster etc. (ed.), *Gnosis* I, ET London 1972; II, 1974; index II, 327 s.v. 'Cross'), contrast abruptly with both Paul and with the synoptic accounts, indeed even with that of John. In connection with the question of the meaning of the cross in earliest Christianity it is best to use these interpretations as a contrast; besides, no one has claimed that there was some kind of unitary 'early Christian theology of the cross' during the first and second centuries AD. Later interpretations had expressly apologetic significance; they are historically conditioned and questionable answers to the reproach of the 'folly' of the cross, see Justin, *Apology* I. 55.8, where διὰ λόγου is to be understood in terms of a rational demonstration. For these manifold apologetic possibilities see H. Rahner, *Greek*

cross which can be seen from Ignatius onwards, in symbolic-allegorical or cosmic terms, has little in common with Paul's λόγος τοῦ σταυροῦ. When Paul began his missionary activity, Christianity was not what it later became at the time of Pliny the Younger or Justin Martyr; it was still a completely unknown Jewish sect in Palestine and the adjoining areas of Syria. It was only a few years since the death of the founder, and personal recollection of events beforehand and afterwards was still alive in the community: I Corinthians 11.23ff.; 15.3ff. (and especially v.6) show that even Paul was not completely unaware of this, despite his 'distance' from the Jesus tradition.[9] Anyone who seeks to deny completely Paul's commitment to the *earthly* figure of the crucified Jesus makes him a docetic theologian.

At the same time, however, this means that for Paul and his contemporaries the cross of Jesus was not a didactic, symbolic or speculative element but a very specific and highly offensive matter which imposed a burden on the earliest Christian missionary preaching. No wonder that the young community in Corinth sought to escape from the *crucified* Christ into the enthusiastic life of the spirit, the enjoyment of heavenly revelations and an assurance of salvation connected with mysteries and sacraments.[10] When in the

---

Myths and Christian Mystery, London 1962, pp.46ff. and Index, p.392, s.v. 'Cross'; also G. Q. Reijners (see bibliography).

[9] This was not so total and so radical as is usually assumed today. Precisely because of the scandal of the cross, it was impossible to be a missionary in the ancient world, proclaiming a crucified messiah and Son of God, without saying something about the activity and the death of this man. Moreover, a need for information is a fundamental human characteristic, especially in connection with a new and revolutionary message. Paul preached to people with a thirst for knowledge, not to stones! P. O. Moe, *Paulus und die evangelische Geschichte*, Leipzig 1912, long ago said what had to be said on the matter. Of course others, like Peter and the missionaries associated with him, had much more to tell about Jesus than Paul had: this could have caused Paul some difficulties on his mission.

[10] It is time to stop talking about 'gnosticism in Corinth'. What happened in the community does not need to be explained in terms of the utterly misleading presupposition of a competing gnostic mission. This never existed, except in the mind of some interpreters. What happened in Corinth can easily be explained in terms of the Hellenistic (and Jewish) milieu of this Greek port and metropolis.

face of this Paul points out to the community which he founded that his preaching of the crucified messiah is a religious 'stumbling block' for the Jews and 'madness' for his Greek hearers, we are hearing in his confession not least the twenty-year experience of the greatest Christian missionary, who had often reaped no more than mockery and bitter rejection with his message of the Lord Jesus, who had died a criminal's death on the tree of shame. This negative reception which was given to the Pauline theology of the cross is continued in the anti-Christian polemic of the ancient world. Walter Bauer was quite right in the remarks with which he concluded his account of the views of the passion of Jesus held by Jewish and pagan opponents of Christianity: 'The enemies of Christianity always referred to the disgracefulness of the death of Jesus with great emphasis and malicious pleasure. A god or son of god dying on the cross! That was enough to put paid to the new religion.'[11] There is an admirable illustration of this in the well-known caricature of a crucified figure with an ass's head from the Palatine with the inscription 'Alexamenos worships god' ('Ἀλεξά-μενος σέβετε [= σέβεται] θεόν). There should be no doubt that this is an anti-Christian parody of the crucified Jesus. The ass's head is not a pointer to some kind of gnostic Seth-worship, but to the Jewish derivation of Christian faith. One of the regular themes of ancient anti-Jewish polemic was that the Jews worshipped an ass in the temple.[12]

Less well-known is another caricature on a tile which comes

---

[11] *Das Leben Jesu im Zeitalter der neutestamentlichen Apokryphen*, Tübingen 1909 (reprinted 1967), 477. Cf. 476: 'How could they have avoided his suffering and dying? Here, if anywhere, their opponents would have been able to make the most devastating criticisms. Jesus had been tried and executed, and not as an innocent man, a new Socrates. On the contrary, he was prosecuted as a criminal, found guilty, sentenced and delivered over to death.'

[12] E. Dinkler, *Signum Crucis* (see bibliography), 150ff.; I. Opelt, 'Esel', *RAC* VI, 592ff.; J.-G. Préaux, 'Deus Christianorum Onocoetes', in *Hommages L. Herrmann*, Brussels-Berchem 1960, 639–54; see also E. Bickermann, 'Ritualmord und Eselskult', *MGWJ* 71, 1927, 171–87; 255–64. The charge of worshipping an ass was raised as early as 200 BC by Mnaseas of Patara. See now M. Stern, *Greek and Latin Authors on Jews and Judaism* I, Jerusalem 1974, 97ff.

from the first half of the fourth century AD and depicts someone
carrying a cross. It was discovered in Oroszvár in Hungary, ancient
Gerulata in the province of Pannonia. The figure is dragging a
Latin cross and his tongue is hanging out under its weight. K. Sági
sees this as 'an interesting testimonial to the reaction against
Christianity, which gradually acquired a dominant position in
parallel with the consolidation of the sole rule of Constantine the
Great'.[13] Here too the pagan who drew the picture has focused his
ridicule on the main point of offence which was caused by the new
religion.

Separated from the particular death of Jesus on the cross, the
Pauline 'word of the cross' would become vague and incomprehensible speculation. At least as far as Paul is concerned, we must
challenge the assertion made in the most recent investigation of the
subject that 'there is no direct route from the historical cross to
theological talk of the "cross"'.[14] The one thing which made Paul's
preaching the offensive 'word of the cross' was the fact that in it the
apostle interpreted the death of Jesus of Nazareth, i.e. of a specific
man, on the cross, as the death of the incarnate Son of God and
Kyrios, proclaiming this event as the eschatological event of salvation for all men. Even the apostle's own suffering is exclusively to
be understood in terms of this historically *unique* event (Rom. 6.10:
ἀπέθανεν ἐφάπαξ). The shame and contempt which the apostle
had to endure is illuminated and explained by the fact of the shameful death of Jesus on the cross. It cannot be detached from this and
be interpreted independently. The enigmatic expression in Colos-
sians 1.24 does not come from the apostle; it is deutero-Pauline. In
my view it already presupposes Paul's martyrdom – perhaps in
Nero's persecutions. Thus for Paul's preaching, the words
σταυρός/σταυροῦν still retained the same original cruelty and abhorrence which was also obvious to the ancient world outside
the Christian tradition, though we find it remote. What Paul says
in I Corinthians 1.17–24 can only be understood against this background. For Paul, therefore, the word has certainly not faded to the

---

[13] K. Sági, 'Darstellung des altchristlichen Kreuzes auf einem
römischen Ziegel', *Acta Antiqua* 16, 1968, (391–400) 400 and pl. 5.
[14] H.-W. Kuhn (see bibliography), 29.

point of becoming a mere 'theological cipher'. Any assertion to this effect merely demonstrates the tenuous link of contemporary exegesis with reality and its insipid and unhistorical character. In other words, the utter offensiveness of the 'instrument for the execution of Jesus' is still to be found in the preaching of Paul.

Thus we can understand all too well how in the pseudo-scientific, popular Platonic arguments used in Gnosticism, this scandal, which deeply offended both religious and philosophical thought in antiquity, was eliminated by the theory that the Son of God had only *seemed* to be crucified. In reality he did not suffer at all. We can see how easily even the orthodox apologist found himself in difficulties here from the laborious argument in Minucius Felix's *Octavius* which has been described on pp. 3f. above. In contrast, worship remained the right place for making public confession of the scandalous paradox of the crucifixion. This is evident not only from the earliest hymns to Christ but also from Melito's *Homily on the Passion*, where it is expressed in polished rhetorical form:[15]

He who hung the earth [in its place] hangs there, he who fixed the heavens is fixed there, he who made all things fast is made fast upon the tree, the Master has been insulted, God has been murdered, the King of Israel has been slain by an Israelitish hand. O strange murder, strange crime! The Master has been treated in unseemly fashion, his body naked, and not even deemed worthy of a covering, that [his nakedness] might not be seen. Therefore the lights [of heaven] turned away, and the day darkened, that it might hide him who was stripped upon the cross.

[15] 96f.; cf. O. Perler, *Méliton de Sardes, Sur la Pâque*, Source Chrétiennes 123, 1966, 194f.

4

Crucifixion as a 'Barbaric' Form of Execution of the Utmost Cruelty

The instances given so far have been an attempt to show that for the men of the ancient world, Greeks, Romans, barbarians and Jews, the cross was not just a matter of indifference, just any kind of death. It was an utterly offensive affair, 'obscene' in the original sense of the word. In the following pages we shall make a further attempt to illuminate the attitude of the ancient world to crucifixion in more detail.

As a rule, books on the subject say that crucifixion began among the Persians. This is true to the extent that we already find numerous references to crucifixion as a form of execution among the Persians in Herodotus, and these can be supplemented by later evidence from Ctesias.[1] However, according to the ancient sources crucifixion was regarded as a mode of execution used by barbarian peoples[2] generally, including the Indians,[3] the Assyrians,[4] the Scythians[5]

[1] Herodotus 1.128.2; 3.125.3; 3.132.2; 3.159.1: Darius has three thousand inhabitants of Babylon crucified; 4.43.2, 7; 6.30.1; 7.194.1f.; Thucydides 1.110.1; also Ctesias (according to Photius) *FGH* 688 F 14.39: Amastris 'crucifies' the Egyptian usurper Inarus on three crosses (presumably this was a matter of impaling his corpse): καὶ ἀνεσταύρισεν μὲν ἐπὶ τρισὶ σταυροῖς; F 14.45: Amastris has the Caunian Alcides crucified; for the treatment of the corpse of the younger Cyrus see Xenophon, *Anabasis* 3.1.17, and Plutarch, *Artaxerxes* 17.5; because of this Parysatis, the queen mother, has the officer who dishonoured Cyrus' body on the orders of Artaxerxes II flayed and crucified, Ctesias F 16.66. Cf. Ezra 6.11 and Haman's cross, Esther 5.14; 7.9f., see below, pp. 84f.

[2] This was already observed by Justus Lipsius, *De Cruce*, Amsterdam 1670, 47ff.: Book I ch. XI is headed '*Apud plerasque gentium cruces fere usitatas*'.

[3] See the threatening letter sent by the Indian king Stabrobates to Semiramis: Diodorus Siculus, *Bibliotheke* 2.18.1.

[4] The Assyrian king Ninus has the Median king Pharnus crucified:

and the Taurians.[6] It was even used by the Celts, who according to Posidonius offered their criminals in this way as a sacrifice to the gods,[7] and later by the Germani[8] and the Britanni,[9] who may well have taken it over from the Romans and combined it with their own forms of punishment. Finally, it was employed by the Numidians and especially by the Carthaginians, who may be the people from whom the Romans learnt it.[10] Crucifixion was not originally a typically Greek penalty; however, the Greeks did have related forms of execution and partially took over crucifixion (see below, pp. 69ff.). Both Greek and Roman historians were fond of stressing *barbarian* crucifixions, and playing down their own use of this form of execution. Mithridates,[11] the arch-enemy of Rome, and two kings of Thrace, the cruel Diegylis and his son Ziselmius, who

---

Diodorus 2.1.10. Lucian, *Iuppiter confutatus* 16: Sardanapalus becomes king and has the valiant (ἀνὴρ ἐνάρετος) Goches crucified. Of course these reports have no historical value. For an older form of execution see the impalement among the Assyrians: *ANEP* 362, 368, and the bas-relief of the storming of Lachish, 373.

[5] Cyrus is crucified by the Scythians: Diodorus Siculus, 2.44.2; cf. Justin, *Epitome* 2.5.6; Tertullian, *Adversus Marcionem* 1.1.3: 'the crosses of the Caucasus' (*crucibus Caucasorum*).

[6] Euripides, *Iphigenia in Tauris* 1429f.: King Thaos wants to have the strangers hurled down from a rock or fastened to a stake (or impaled). For the Thracians see n. 12 below.

[7] Diodorus Siculus 5.32.6: καὶ περὶ τὰς θυσίας ἐκτόπως ἀσεβοῦσι · τοὺς γὰρ κακούργους . . . ἀνασκολοπίζουσι τοῖς θεοῖς . . . (And they are monstrously impious in their sacrifices; for they crucify evildoers for their gods.)

[8] Tacitus, *Annals* 1.61.4; 4.72.3, but cf. *Germania* 12.1: *proditores et transfugas arboribus suspendunt* (they hang traitors and deserters on trees). See also Dio Cassius 54.20.4; Florus, *Epitome* 2.30 = 4.12.24.

[9] Tacitus, *Annals* 14.33.2: *sed caedes patibula, ignes cruces, tamquam reddituri supplicium, et praerepta interim ultione, festinabant* (they made haste with slaughter and the gibbet, with fires and crosses, as though the day of reckoning must come, but only after revenge had been snatched in the interval). Cf. Dio Cassius 62. 7.2 and 11.4.

[10] Numidians: Sallust, *Bellum Iugurthinum* 14.15; Caesar, *Bellum Africum* 66. Carthaginians: Polybius 1.11.5; 24.6; 79.4f.; 86.4; Diodorus Siculus 25.5.2; 10.2; 26.23.1; Livy 22.13.9; 28.37.2; 38.48.13; Valerius Maximus 2.7 ext. 1: Justin, *Epitome* 18.7.15; Silius Italicus, *Punica* 1.181; 2.435f.

[11] Appian, *Mithridatic Wars* 97; cf. Valerius Maximus 9.2, ext. 3.

was even worse, were cited as deterrent examples in the Hellenistic period.[12]

A particular problem is posed by the fact that the *form* of crucifixion varied considerably. Above all, there is not always a clear distinction between the crucifixion of the victim while he is still alive and the display of the corpse of someone who has been executed in a different fashion. In both cases it was a matter of subjecting the victim to the utmost indignity. As a rule, Herodotus uses the verb ἀνασκολοπίζειν of living men and ἀνασταυροῦν of corpses. Ctesias, on the other hand, uses only ἀνασταυρίζειν for both. The common factor in all these verbs is that the victim – living or dead – was either nailed or bound to a stake, σκόλοψ or σταυρός. The texts do not always make it clear whether cross-beams were used here. Polycrates of Samos, for instance, the most famous example in antiquity, was not crucified in the strict sense; he was lured by the satrap Oroites into Persian territory, killed 'in an unspeakable (cruel) way' and his body fastened to a stake: ἀποκτείνας δέ μιν οὐκ ἀξίως ἀπηγήσιος Ὀροίτης ἀνεσταύρωσε (Herodotus, *History* 3.125.3). Nevertheless, later tradition saw him as the prototype of the crucified victim whose fate represented a sudden change from supreme good fortune to the uttermost disaster.[13] After Herodotus the words ἀνασκολοπίζειν and ἀνασταυροῦν became synonyms. Josephus, for example, uses only (ἀνα)σταυροῦν, while Philo on the other hand uses only ἀνασκολοπίζειν for the same thing. However, neither of the two verbs appears in the only detailed account of a crucifixion given by Herodotus. According to him, the Athenian general Xanthippus had the satrap Artayctes executed for religious offences at the very place where Xerxes had once built a bridge over the Hellespont: "They

[12] Diodorus Siculus 33.15.1: 34/35.12.1: impalements are recorded of the father and crucifixions of the son.

[13] Cicero, *De finibus* 5.92; Valerius Maximus 6.9 ext.2; Fronto, *Epistula de bello Parthico* (van den Hout I, pp.208f.); Lucian, *Charon* 14; Dio Chrysostom, *Oratio* 17 (67).15; cf. also the interpretation in Philo, *De providentia* fr. 2.24f., following Eusebius, *Praeparatio Evangelica* 8.14.24f. (Mras, GCS 43.1, pp.468f.), and the Armenian version 2.25: 'by which he met a gruesome fate'. For Philo his crucifixion is the ultimate punishment for his wicked life.

nailed him to planks and hung him there ([πρὸς] σανίδας προσ-
πασσαλεύσαντες ἀνεκρέμασαν). And they stoned Artayctes' son
before his eyes.'[14] We have very few more detailed descriptions,
and they come only from Roman times: the passion narratives in the
gospels are in fact the most detailed of all. No ancient writer wanted
to dwell too long on this cruel procedure.

Even in the Roman empire, where there might be said to be
some kind of 'norm' for the course of the execution (it included a
flogging beforehand, and the victim often carried the beam to the
place of execution, where he was nailed to it with outstretched
arms, raised up and seated on a small wooden peg),[15] the form of
execution could vary considerably: crucifixion was a punishment
in which the caprice and sadism of the executioners were given full
rein. All attempts to give a perfect description of *the* crucifixion in
archaeological terms are therefore in vain; there were too many
different possibilities for the executioner. Seneca's testimony speaks
for itself:

> I see crosses there, not just of one kind but made in many different
> ways: some have their victims with head down to the ground; some
> impale their private parts; others stretch out their arms on the gibbet.
>
> (*Video istic cruces, non unius quidem generis, sed aliter ab aliis fabricatas:
> capite quidam conuersos in terram suspendere, alii per obscena stipitem
> egerunt, alii brachia patibulo explicuerunt.*)[16]

From Josephus we have an eyewitness account of the fate of Jewish
fugitives who attempted to escape from besieged Jerusalem:

> When they were going to be taken (by the Romans), they were forced
> to defend themselves, and after they had fought they thought it too

[14] Herodotus 9.120, cf. 7.33: ζῶντα πρὸς σανίδα διεπασσάλευσαν. I. Barkan
(see bibliography), 69f., conjectures an instance of '*apotympanismos*' here,
see pp. 69ff. below.

[15] For the *sedile* see H. Fulda (see bibliography), 149ff.; for nailing,
J. Blinzler (see bibliography), 375ff. (ET 264f.). Cf. below p. 31 n. 25.

[16] *Dialogue* 6 (*De consolatione ad Marciam*) 20.3; cf. *Martyria Petri et
Pauli* 60 (Lipsius I, p. 170). Y. Yadin, 'Epigraphy' (see bibliography),
believes that epigraphical and anatomical evidence must lead us to suppose
that the crucified figure discovered at Jerusalem was fastened to the cross
upside down. For 'spitting' the victim as a variation see p. 69 n. 1 below.
Apuleius, *Metamorphoses* 8.22.4f., describes another kind of torture. Cf.
Suidae Lexicon (Adler III, p. 223.10ff.) s.v. Κύφωνες: a slow death at the
pillory similar to crucifixion.

late to make any supplications for mercy: so they were first whipped, and then tormented with all sorts of tortures, before they died and were then crucified before the wall of the city (μαστιγούμενοι δὴ καὶ προβασανιζόμενοι τοῦ θανάτου πᾶσαν αἰκίαν ἀνεσταυροῦντο τοῦ τείχους ἀντικρύ). Titus felt pity for them, but as their number – given as up to five hundred a day – was too great for him to risk either letting them go or putting them under guard, he allowed his soldiers to have their way, especially as he hoped that the gruesome sight of the countless crosses might move the besieged to surrender: 'So the soldiers, out of the rage and hatred they bore the prisoners, nailed those they caught, in different postures, to the crosses, by way of jest (προσήλουν . . . ἄλλον ἄλλῳ σχήματι πρὸς χλεύην), and their number was so great that there was not enough room for the crosses and not enough crosses for the bodies.'[17]

The same sort of thing probably happened on the direct instructions of the emperor at the time of the first persecution of Christians by Nero in Rome. This is probably the way in which the famous and disputed passage in Tacitus, *Annals* 15.44.4, is to be interpreted:

> *Et pereuntibus addita ludibria, ut ferarum tergis contecti laniatu canum interirent, aut crucibus adfixi atque flammati, ubi defecisset dies, in usu(m) nocturni luminis urerentur.*

(And additional derision accompanied their end: they were covered with wild beasts' skins and torn to death by dogs; or they were fastened on crosses and, when daylight faded, were burned to serve as lamps by night.)

In other words, the *aut crucibus adfixi atque flammati* is not to be deleted as a gloss; rather, crucifixion was the basic punishment to

---

[17] Josephus, *BJ* 5.449–51. For mass crucifixions in Judaea see also *BJ* 2.75 (*Antiquitates* 17.295): Varus before Jerusalem 4 BC; cf. also 2.241: crucifixion of all the Jews taken prisoner by Cumanus; according to *Antiquitates* 20.129 the chief offenders among the Samaritans and the Jews were crucified. Cf. *BJ* 2.253: Felix has a large number of 'robbers' crucified; 2.306, 308: crucifixions by Florus in Jerusalem. A Jewish prisoner at Jotapata (3.321) πρὸς πᾶσαν αἰκίαν βασάνων ἀντέσχεν καὶ μηδὲν διὰ πυρὸς ἐξερευνῶσι τοῖς πολεμίοις περὶ τῶν ἔνδον εἰπὼν ἀνεσταυρώθη τοῦ θανάτου καταμειδιῶν (Though tortured in all kinds of ways and passed through the fire, he told the enemy nothing of those within, and as he was crucified, smiled at death). 5.289: Titus has a Jew, captured during a foray, crucified in front of the walls, εἴ τι πρὸς τὴν ὄψιν ἔνδοθεν οἱ λοιποὶ καταπλαγέντες (to see whether the rest of them would be frightened). Cf. p.85 n.5 below.

which the *addita ludibria* were added.[18] Dio Cassius confirms Nero's cruel habits in crucifixions – though without, of course, mentioning Christians, about whom he is silent throughout his work (63.13.2).

We already learn from Plato's Gorgias that the crucifixion of a criminal was often preceded by various kinds of torture. There Polus tries to refute Socrates by a particularly horrifying example – which is nevertheless probably based on the political realities of the time:

> If a man is caught in a criminal plot to make himself tyrant, and when caught is put to the rack and mutilated and has his eyes burnt out and after himself suffering and seeing his wife and children suffer many other signal outrages of various kinds is finally crucified (τὸ ἔσχατον ἀνασταυρωθῇ)[19] or burned in a coat of pitch, will he be happier than if he escaped arrest, established himself as a tyrant and lived the rest of his life a sovereign in his state, doing what he pleased, an object of envy and felicitation among citizens and strangers alike? (473bc)

Socrates rejects the alternative as a false one, 'for of two miserable creatures one cannot be the happier', though he goes on to say that the one who becomes a tyrant is more wretched than the one who dies under torture – a reply which draws scornful laughter from his opponent (473de).

Plato takes up the theme again in the famous example of the innocent sufferer (*Republic* 361e–362a), but now applies it in the opposite way, which gives his argument a prophetic urgency. Glaucon compares the completely unjust man with the completely just man (360e). Through his cunning and lack of scruple the unjust man will acquire power and riches and with them the appearance of the utmost uprightness, whereas the completely just

---

[18] See also Koestermann, op. cit. (p.3 n.3 above), 257, following Capocci, who conjectures similar happenings to those depicted in Josephus, *BJ* 5.451, or Philo, *In Flaccum* 72.85. For the rich arsenal of atrocities of this kind see also Seneca, *Dialogue* 5 (= *De ira* 3) 3.6.

[19] Philo, *In Flaccum* 72: after all the preceding tortures ἡ τελευταία καὶ ἔφεδρος τιμωρία σταυρὸς ἦν (the last and supreme punishment was the cross). Cf. Eusebius, *Historia Ecclesiae* 3.32.6: καὶ ἐπὶ πολλαῖς ἡμέραις αἰκιζόμενος . . . καὶ ἐκελεύσθη σταυρωθῆναι (He was tortured for many days and orders were given for him to be crucified).

man will be looked upon and treated as an unjust man and finally –
here Glaucon apologizes for the vividness and realism of his
language – will be tortured to death:

> The just man will have to be scourged, racked, fettered, blinded, and
> finally, after the uttermost suffering, he will be impaled (τελευτῶν
> πάντα κακὰ παθὼν ἀνασχινδυλευθήσεται), and so will learn his lesson
> that not to be but to seem to be just is what we ought to desire.

Plato certainly has Socrates in mind as the example of the completely just man who cares nothing for the views of his fellow-
citizens. It is therefore all the more striking that in contrast to the
'humane' execution of Socrates he envisages the just man being
killed in an extremely barbarous fashion which was quite out of the
ordinary for Athenian citizens. It is significant that Christian
writers – e.g. Clement of Alexandria and the author of the *Acta
Apollonii* – are the first deliberately to take up again the theme of
the crucified just man in Plato. Where other ancient authors
possibly allude to it – with the exception of Lucian (see p. 83
below) – they leave out any account of crucifixion, which was
offensive to them.[20] As at a later date Demosthenes, when defend-
ing himself against a trumped-up charge of murder (*Oratio* 21.105,
against Meidias), describes 'being nailed up' (προσηλοῦσθαι) as the
worst form of execution, we must assume that crucifixion or similar
forms of execution were not completely foreign even to the Greeks
(see pp. 69ff. below).

The combination of crucifixion and torture beforehand was also
customary among the Carthaginians and in the relatively 'normal'

---

[20] Plato is probably thinking of a particularly cruel form of '*apotympanismos*' (see below, pp. 70f.). For Christian interpretation since the *Acta
Apollonii* 39f. and Clement of Alexandria, *Stromateis* 5.108.2f.; 4.52.1f.,
see E. Benz (see bibliography), 31ff. Allusions to just men suffering without crucifixion are found in Maximus of Tyre, *Dialexeis* 12.10 (Hobein,
pp. 156f.); Cicero, *De republica* 3.27, following Carneades; cf. Seneca,
Dialogue 2 (*De constantia sapientis*) 15.1. H. Hommel, 'Die Satorformel
und ihr Ursprung', *ThViat* 1952, (108–180) 124–33, supplements and
corrects Benz, pointing to Macedonian parallels, see p. 72 n. 12 below.
Significantly enough, the rare word ἀνασκινδα(υ)λεύειν only reappears in
the church fathers with express reference to Plato, see Eusebius, *Praeparatio Evangelica* 12.10.4; Theodoret, *Graecarum Affectionum Curatio* 8
(PG 83,1012).

course of execution among the Romans; at the least, a flogging was carried out before the execution.[21] However, the torture which came first probably helped to shorten the actual torments of crucifixion, which were caused above all by the duration of the suffering. A later text explicitly states that hanging on the gallows (*furca*), which gradually took the place of crucifixion after the time of Constantine and the later Christian emperors of the fourth century, was essentially a more humane punishment:

> But hanging is a lesser penalty than the cross. For the gallows kills the victim immediately, whereas the cross tortures for a long time those who are fixed to it.
>
> (*sed patibuli* (= *furca*) *minor poena quam crucis. Nam patibulum adpoenos statim exanimat, crux autem subfixos diu cruciat.*)[22]

Following Livy (30.43.13), Valerius Maximus (2.7.12) says that the older Scipio punished Roman deserters at the end of the Second

[21] See J. Blinzler (see bibliography), 321ff. (ET 222ff.), who refers to *Digest* 48.19.8.3, according to which many people even died during the torture. Cf. Dionysius of Halicarnassus, *Antiquitates Romanae* 5.51.3: μάστιξι καὶ βασάνοις αἰκισθέντες ἀνεσκολοπίσθησαν ἅπαντες (after being tormented with whips and tortures, all were crucified), and 7.69.1f.: Diodorus Siculus 18.16.3, see p. 74 n. 15 below. Nero was threatened with flogging as a death penalty *more maiorum* (Suetonius, *Nero* 49.2): *nudi hominis cervicem inseri furcae, corpus virgis ad necem caedi* (the criminal was stripped, fastened by the neck in a fork, and then beaten to death with rods). According to the saga it was carried out publicly as early as by King Tarquinius Superbus: Dio Cassius 2, fr. 11.6; the victims were bound naked to the stake before the eyes of their fellow-citizens and flogged to death: ἐν τοῖς τοῦ δήμου ὅμμασι σταυροῖς τε γυμνοὺς προσέδησεν καὶ ῥάβδοις αἰκισάμενος ἀπέκτεινεν (Boissevain I, p. 27). Scipio Africanus maior acted in this way in Spain to preserve military discipline (Dio Cassius 16 after Zonaras 9.10.8 [I, p. 251]), and C. F. Fimbrias used the punishment in Macedonia in the Mithridatic war (Dio Cassius 30–35, fr. 104.6 [I, p. 348]); the last Hasmonean king Antigonus was humiliated in this way in 38 BC and then executed with the axe, 'which no other king had endured from the Romans' (Dio Cassius 49.22.6). Cf. M. Fuhrmann, 'Verbera', *PW* Suppl. IX (1589–97) 1590ff. For the combination of flogging and crucifixion see Livy 22.13.9; 28.37.3: *laceratosque verberibus cruci adfigi iussit* (when they had been beaten with lashes he ordered them to be fastened to the cross).

[22] Isidore of Seville, *Etymologia* 5.27.34 (Lindsay). Apuleius, *Metamorphoses* 8.22.5, comes near to a crucifixion: a slave is tied to a tree and slowly tortured to death (*per longi temporis cruciatum*). See Fulda (see bibliography), 115f.

Punic War more harshly (*grauius*) than the Latin allies: he crucified
the former as renegades and traitors, but beheaded the latter as
treacherous allies.

> *hos enim tamquam patriae fugitiuos crucibus adfixit, illos tamquam*
> *perfidos socios securi percussit.*

In Epistle 101 to Lucilius, Seneca makes a spirited defence
against Maecenas of the possibility of suicide as the last way to freedom in unbearable suffering. In the form of a verse, Maecenas
compares the illnesses and griefs of his old age with the torments
of the crucified man; nevertheless, he is determined to hold on to
life at any price:

> Fashion me with a palsied hand,
> weak of foot and a cripple.
> Build upon me a crook-backed hump,
> Shake my teeth till they rattle.
> All is well if my life remains.
> Save, oh, save it, I pray you,
> Though I sit on the piercing cross.
>
> (*Debilem facito manu, debilem pede coxo,*
> *Tuber adstrue gibberum, lubricos quate dentes;*
> *Vita dum superest, benest; hanc mihi, vel acuta*
> *Si sedeam cruce, sustine.*)

For Seneca, on the other hand, a life which can be compared with
the torments of hanging on the cross, with only a peg to support
the body, and in which the only comfort is the outcome of the
execution, death, is no longer worth living:

> Is it worth while to weigh down on one's own wound and hang
> impaled on a gibbet in order to postpone something which is the
> balm of troubles, the end of punishment?
>
> (*Est tanti vulnus suum premere et patibulo pendere districtum, dum*
> *differat id, quod est in malis optimum, supplicii finem?*)

A lengthy process of dying is no longer worthy of the name of 'life'.
There follows a description of the gradual expiry of the victim of
crucifixion which is unique in ancient literature:

> Can anyone be found who would prefer wasting away in pain dying
> limb by limb, or letting out his life drop by drop, rather than expiring

once for all? Can any man be found willing to be fastened to the accursed tree, long sickly, already deformed, swelling with ugly weals on shoulders and chest, and drawing the breath of life amid long-drawn-out agony? He would have many excuses for dying even before mounting the cross.

(Invenitur aliquis, qui velit inter supplicia tabescere et perire membratim et totiens per stilicidia emittere animam quam semel exhalare? Invenitur, qui velit adactus ad illud infelix lignum, iam debilis, iam pravus et in foedum scapularum ac pectoris tuber elisus, cui multae moriendi causae etiam citra crucem fuerant, trahere animam tot tormenta tracturam?)[23]

In view of the evidence from antiquity, it is incomprehensible that some scholars could have stated recently that crucifixion was 'by nature a bloodless form of execution'.[24] Statements of this kind, which go against all the historical evidence, are prompted by the questionable tendency to draw a dividing line between New Testament remarks about the bloody sacrificial death of Jesus and the Pauline *theologia crucis*, which is still held in high esteem. It should be noted that in Roman times not only was it the rule to nail the victim by both hands and feet,[25] but that the flogging

[23] Cf. *Dialogue* 3 (*De ira* 1) 2.2: *alium in cruce membra diffindere* ('another to have his limbs stretched upon the cross'), as a climax at the end of an enumeration of gruesome forms of death; *Dialogue* 5 (*De ira* 3), 3.6: *eculei et fidiculae et ergastula et cruces et circumdati defossis corporibus ignes . . . uaria poenarum, lacerationes membrorum* (the torture horse, the cord, the gaol, the cross and fires encircling living bodies implanted in the ground and the different kinds of punishments . . . the rending of limbs); see also Valerius Maximus 6.9 ext. 5, the macabre account of the crucified Polycrates; Cicero, *in Pisonem* 42: *An ego, si te et Gabinium cruci suffixos viderem, maiore adficerer laetitia ex corporis vestri laceratione quam adficior ex famae?* (Or if I were to see you and Gabinius fixed to a cross, should I feel a greater joy at the laceration of your bodies than I do at that of your reputations?); Apuleius, *Metamorphoses* 6.32.1: *et patibuli cruciatum, cum canes et vultures intima protrahent viscera* (the torment of the gibbet, where dogs and vultures shall drag out her innermost entrails).

[24] E. Brandenburger (see bibliography), 18; cf. id., 'Kreuz', *TBLNT* II, 1, 1969, 826f.: 'Indeed crucifixion is . . . by its very nature (!) a bloodless affair'. For an answer I can only refer to Josephus, *Antiquitates* 19.94. Cf. also J. Jeremias, *The Eucharistic Words of Jesus*, London and New York 1966, 223, who puts forward the same view as Brandenburger, but from a very different perspective.

[25] J. Blinzler (see bibliography), 361f., 377ff. (ET 250, 264f.); J. W. Hewitt, 'The Use of Nails in Crucifixion', *HTR* 25, 1932, 29–45; cf. *inter alia* Philo, *De posteritate Caini* 61; *De somniis* 2.213; Achilles Tatius,

which was a stereotyped part of the punishment would make the blood flow in streams. Binding the victim to the cross only with bonds remained the exception.[26] Presumably Jesus was so weakened by loss of blood that he was unable to carry the beam of the cross to the place of execution; this is also the best explanation of his relatively speedy death. The 'ugly weals on shoulders and chest' in Seneca's macabre description are probably a reference to the consequences of the flogging.

The evidence from Seneca and elsewhere also shows that even where crucifixion is only used as a simile or metaphor, its gruesome reality could very well be before the eyes of the writer. In essentials, this will also be the case with Christian talk of the cross up to the time of the edict of toleration in AD 311. Not only were crosses set up all over the empire, but Christians themselves will either have been executed on the cross or at least will have to have reckoned with crucifixion or similar punishment.[27]

2.37.3; Plutarch, *Moralia* 499D; Pliny the Elder, *Historia Naturalis* 28.41, 46; Ps. Manetho, *Apotelesmatica* 4.199; 1.149; Seneca, *Dialogue* 7 (*De vita beata*) 19.3; Lucan, *De Bello Civili* 6.543–7; Apuleius, *Metamorphoses* 3.17.4; Galen, *De usu partium* 12.11 (Kühn IV, p.45); Artemidorus, *Oneirocriticon* 2.56; Lucian, *Prometheus* 1.2; *Dialogus deorum* 5(1).1 (see above p.11 n.1). In Xenophon of Ephesus, *Ephesiaca* 4.23, binding to the cross is mentioned as an Egyptian custom for reasons connected with the narrative, and therefore as an exception; but cf. Chariton 4.3.6: the hero is not to be wounded at his crucifixion. See now also the discovery of a skeleton of a crucified man in Jerusalem in which the nail is still in the heel bones: N. Haas, 'Anthropological Observations on the Skeletal Remains from Giv'at ha-Mivtar', *IEJ* 20, 1970, (38–59) 49ff. and P. Ducrey, 'Note' (see bibliography).

[26] Fulda (see bibliography) 161ff. saw this as an intensification. Pliny the Elder, *Historia Naturalis* 28.46, and the witch in Lucan, *De Bello Civili* 6.543f., 547, know of the magical use of nails and bonds employed at a crucifixion.

[27] Cf. Justin, *Dialogue with Trypho* 110.4; Tertullian, *Apologeticus* 12.3: *crucibus et stipitibus imponitis Christianos* (You put Christians on crosses and stakes); 50.12; *Ad nationes* 1.3.8; 1.6.6; 1.18.1; *De anima* 1.6; 56.8, etc. Eusebius, *Historia Ecclesiae* 2.25.5; 3.32.6: Simeon son of Clopas of Jerusalem under Trajan according to Hegesippus; 8.8.10. Further instances in P. Garnsey (see bibliography), 127f. n.10.

5

Crucifixion as the Supreme Roman Penalty

All this also helps us to understand how in his speech against Verres Cicero could already describe crucifixion as the *summum supplicium*.[1] The continuing legal tradition which can be seen here is brought to an end by the jurist Julius Paulus about AD 200. In the *Sententiae* compiled from his works towards AD 300, the *crux* is put at the head of the three *summa supplicia*. It is followed, in descending order, by *cremptio* (burning) and *decollatio* (decapitation). In the lists of penalties given in the sources, *damnatio ad bestias* often takes the place of decapitation as an aggravated penalty. This shows that *decollatio* was not always included among the *summa supplicia*. Similarly, in the Greek East we find during the early imperial period in a Lycian inscription, in Philo and in an edict of the Egyptian prefect the threat of the ἀνωτάτω τιμωρία or κόλασις but without a further mention of crucifixion.[2] At the same

---

[1] *In Verrem* 2.5.168: *Adservasses hominem* (P. Gavius) *custodiis Mamertinorum tuorum, vinctum clausum habuisses, dum Panhormo Raecius veniret* ('You would have kept him with your Messinian friends, chained and locked up, till Raecius arrived from Panhormus', in order to prove that the accused was a Roman citizen); *cognosceret hominem, aliquid de summo supplicio remitteres* ('should he identify the man you would no doubt lessen the extreme penalty'). 169: Verres' crime is less against Gavius than again Rome and Italy: *Italia autem alumnum suum servitutis extremo summoque supplicio adfixum videret* (Italy might see her son as he hung there suffer the worst extremes of tortures inflicted upon slaves). Cf. Philo, *In Flaccum* 72 (see p. 27 n. 19); Florus, *Epitome* 1.18 = 2.2.25: *nec ultimo sive carceris seu crucis supplicio* (nor by the final punishment of prison or cross), and Cicero's rhetorical questions, *In Pisonem* 44.

[2] Paulus, *Sententiae* 5.17.2 (Krüger, *Collectio librorum iuris anteiustiniani* II, p. 126); Minucius Felix, *Octavius* 9.4 (above, p. 3). For an enumeration of these supreme penalties see also Sallust, *Bellum Iugurthinum* 14.15;

time the *Sententiae* give catalogues of crimes which are punished by crucifixion, including desertion to the enemy, the betraying of secrets, incitement to rebellion, murder, prophecy about the welfare of rulers (*de salute dominorum*), nocturnal impiety (*sacra impia nocturna*), magic (*ars magica*), serious cases of the falsification of wills, etc.[3] Here we can see the further development of capital punishment during the later empire. Of course because of its harshness, crucifixion was almost always inflicted only on the lower class (*humiliores*); the upper class (*honestiores*) could reckon with more 'humane' punishment. Here we have a real case of 'class justice'. The class distinction became particularly significant after the introduction of universal Roman citizenship by Caracalla; however, it had already been in effect previously, especially among the

---

Seneca the Elder, *Controversiae* exc. 8.4; Lucan, *De Bello Civili* 10.365; Apuleius, *Metamorphoses* 6.31.1; 32.1; Xenophon, *Ephesiaca* 4.62f.; Justin, *Dialogue with Trypho* 110.4; cf. pp. 77f. n. 26. For the *summa supplicia* as 'aggravated forms of the death penalty' see P. Garnsey (see bibliography), 124. Professor Louis Robert has called my attention to an inscription, a better reading of which has recently been published, which comes from Myra in Lycia and from the time of Claudius. According to this the imperial legate, of senatorial rank, who was entrusted with the administration of the new province, scourged a slave who had accepted some doubtful documents for the city archives, although he had been warned against this, and threatened that if he offended again he would be punished most severely: 'and with a demonstration of this kind (i.e. the flogging), I made it clear to him that if he offended against the administration again . . . I would compel the rest of the city slaves to forget their earlier negligence not only with blows but with the supreme penalty against him (οὐ πληγαῖς μόνον, ἀλλὰ καὶ τῆι ἀ[νω]τάτωι κολάσει αὐτοῦ); M. Wörrle, 'Zwei neue griechische Inschriften aus Myra zur Verwaltung Lykiens in der Kaiserzeit', in: *Myra*, Istanbuler Forschungen 30, 1975, (254–300) 256 lines 14–19. For the ἀνωτάτω τιμωρία see op. cit., 281 n. 681: Philo, *In Flaccum* 126; L. Mitteis/U. Wilcken, *Grundzüge und Chrestomathie der Papyruskunde*, Berlin 1912, I, 2, no. 439 = E. M. Smallwood, *Documents Illustrating the Principates of Gaius, Claudius and Nero*, Cambridge 1967, no. 381: edict of the prefect of Egypt of 29.4.42 AD against soldiers who oppressed the populace: κατὰ τούτου τῇ ἀνωτάτω χρήσομαι τειμωρίᾳ. In the Myra inscription the reading quoted above is to be preferred to an earlier one which presupposes a reference to crucifixion here.

[3] Paulus, *Sententiae* 5.19.2; 21.4; 23.2, 16; 25.1; 30b.1. See also U. Brasiello, *La repressione penale in diritto romano*, Naples 1937, 248ff.; P. Garnsey, op. cit., 122–31; A. Zestermann (see bibliography), 25f.

foreigners (*peregrini*).[4] The important thing here is that *crux, bestiae, ignis* were regarded as aggravated punishments and not as mere variables.[5] In terms of severity, crucifixion can only be compared with the 'popular entertainment' of throwing victims to the wild beasts (*bestiis obici*); however, this was not listed among the *summa supplicia* as 'the regular forms of execution . . ., because whether or not it was carried out depended on the chance circumstance that such a popular festival had been arranged . . .'.[6] By comparison crucifixion was a much more common punishment; it could be carried out almost anywhere, whereas *bestiis obici* required a city arena and the necessary facilities. Of course, crucifixion too could serve as a 'popular entertainment'; according to Philo (*In Flaccum* 72.84f.) this was the case with the torture and subsequent crucifixion of Jews in Alexandria by the prefect Flaccus. It could also happen in mime as in the representation of the execution of the robber chief Laureolus, at which a great deal of artificial blood flowed; both these instances date from the time of Caligula (AD 37–41).[7] Juvenal wished that the actor Lentulus were on a real cross in this fearsome piece; it was an abomination to the satirist that the actor, as a member of the upper class, should debase himself by such a performance (8.187f.). Under Domitian a real criminal seems to have played the part of the robber chief: we read how he was hung on a cross and torn to pieces by a Scottish bear (Martial, *Liber Spectaculorum* 7):

Laureolus, hanging on no unreal cross, gave up his vitals defenceless

[4] For the aggravation of capital punishment see E. Levy, 'Die römische Kapitalstrafe', in *Gesammelte Schriften* II, 1963, 325–78, esp. 353ff.; cf. id., 'Gesetz und Richter im kaiserlichen Strafrecht, Erster Teil', ibid., (433–508) 487f. Cf. also G. Cardascia, 'L'apparition dans le droit des classes d'"honestiores" et d'"humiliores"', *RHDF* 58, 1950, 305–36, 461–85; for penal law see 319ff.

[5] Thus U. Brasiello, op. cit., 246ff., 260ff.; endorsed by G. Cardascia, op. cit., 321 n.7. Brasiello (257) defines the *summum supplicium* as 'massima tortura' or 'pene con cui si tormenta nel modo più doloroso il condannato', but see P. Garnsey (see bibliography), 122f.

[6] T. Mommsen (see bibliography), 927.

[7] Josephus, *Antiquitates* 19.94; cf. Suetonius, *Caligula* 57.4; Tertullian, *Adversus Valentinianos* 14.4, cf. J. G. Griffith, *Mnemosyne* 15, 1962, 256ff. For torture, crucifixion and burning in the arena see also Seneca, *Epistulae morales* 14.5; cf. p. 27 n. 18 above.

to a Caledonian bear. His mangled limbs lived, though the parts
dripped blood and in all his body was nowhere a body's shape.

(nuda Caledonio sic viscera praebuit urso
non falsa pendens in cruce Laureolus
vivebant laceri membris stillantibus artus
inque omni nusquam corpore corpus erat.)

A similarly cruel form of execution was devised for the slave girl
Blandina during the persecution of Christians in Lyons.[8] Nero is
said to have covered himself with the hide of a wild animal and to
have tormented the victims hanging on crosses (Dio Cassius
63.13.2). While Martial depicts with satisfaction (or even with an
attack of bad conscience) the crimes which may have been committed by those hanging on the cross, Varro had long since denounced
the barbarism of such a form of punishment:[9]

> Are we barbarians because we fasten the innocent to the cross, and
> are you not barbarians because you throw the guilty to the wild
> beasts?
>
> *(nos barbari quod innocentes in gabalum suffigimus homines; uos non*
> *barbari quod noxios obicitis bestiis?)*

People were only too well aware of the particular cruelty of this
form of punishment[10] – at one point (*In Verrem* II.5.162) Cicero

---

[8] Eusebius, *Historia Ecclesiae* 5.1.41: ἐπὶ ξύλου κρεμασθεῖσα προύκειτο βορὰ
τῶν ... θηρίων · ἢ καὶ διὰ τοῦ βλέπεσθαι σταυροῦ σχήματι κρεμαμένη ... (suspen-
ded on a stake, she was exposed as food to wild beasts. To look at her, as
she hung cross-wise ...).

[9] Menippus, fr. 24 (p. 96, J.-P. Cèbe, *Varron, Satires Ménippées*, Rome
1972). Like *crux* (above, p. 9 n. 21), *gabalus* is also a taunt: *Anthologia
Latina* 801.2M = *Scriptores Historiae Augustae* 15 (Iulius Capitolinus,
Macrinus) 11.6.

[10] Apuleius, *Metamorphoses* 1.15.4: *sed saevitia cruci me reservasse*
(cruelly kept me for the cross); cf. Seneca, *Epistulae morales* 14.5: *et quic-
quid aliud praeter haec commenta saeuitia est* (and all the other contrivances
devised by cruelty). *Scriptores Historiae Augustae* 6 (Vulcacius Gallicanus,
Avidius Cassius) 4.1f.: *multa extant crudelitatis potius quam severitatis eius
indicia, nam primum milites ... in illis ipsis locis, in quibus peccaverant, in
crucem sustulit* (there are many indications of savagery rather than strict-
ness, for in the first place ... he crucified the soldiers in the spot where they
had committed their crimes). Cf. *Scriptores Historiae Augustae* 12 (Iulius
Capitolinus, *Clodius Albinus*) 11.6; 19 (Iulius Capitolinus, *Maximini*)
8.5ff.: *tam crudelis fuit ... alios in crucem sublatos* (so cruel that he hung
men on the cross); Cicero, *Philippicae* 13.21: *hostis taeterrimus omnibus*

succinctly calls it 'that plague' (*istam pestem*); however, it is almost impossible to find a protest against its use in principle. Cicero twice protested against the crucifixion of Roman citizens, once acting for the prosecution and once for the defence, but he was concerned with quite specific individual instances. He may have accused Verres of having crucified a Roman citizen, P. Gavius, but at the same time he objected that Verres had handed back to their masters a large number of slaves who were suspected of conspiracy to rebellion *instead of* crucifying them.[11] And while the Stoic Seneca ascribes the abomination of crucifixion and other tortures to the worst of all passions, anger, he takes it for granted that criminals have to be executed in this way.[12] We can see here, in the educated world of antiquity, a schizophrenia similar to that which we encounter in connection with the use of the death penalty in large areas of modern society.

It is certainly the case that the Roman world was largely unanimous that crucifixion was a horrific, disgusting business. There is therefore hardly any mention of it in inscriptions; the only evidence from Latin epigraphy which I can find is the pious wish, 'May you be nailed to the cross' (*in cruce figarus* = *figaris*).[13] As far

---

bonis cruces ac tormenta minitatur (a most hideous enemy is threatening all good men with crucifixion and torture). Justin, *Epitome* 22.7.8: the crucifixion of Bomilcar demonstrates the *crudelitas* of the Carthaginians; Diodorus Siculus 26.23.1: the crucifixion of the members of a Numidian tribe by the Carthaginians is described as ὠμότης.

[11] *In Verrem* II.5.9–13: *hos ad supplicium iam more maiorum traditos ex media morte eripere ac liberare ausus es, ut, quam damnatis crucem servis fixeras, hanc indemnatis videlicet civibus Romanis reservares?* (the quotation is from 12). (When they were already delivered over, in the manner prescribed by tradition, to suffer execution, did you dare to save them, to pluck them from the very jaws of death, intending no doubt that the gallows you set up for the slaves who had been convicted should be kept for Roman citizens who had not?)

[12] Seneca, *Dialogue* 5 (*De ira 3*) 3.6; but cf. *De clementia* 1.23: piety (here the love of parents) was at its lowest ebb after the sack (the ancient punishment for parricide or matricide) became a more frequent sight than the cross (*pessimo loco pietas fuit postquam saepius culleos quam cruces*). Even when the state is to be praised, in which men are rarely punished (*in qua . . . raro homines puniuntur*), one cannot completely avoid cruel punishments. See also below, p. 60.

[13] *CIL IV*, 2082, from Pompeii (strada di Olconio).

as I can tell, the words *crux* or *patibulum* do not appear in Caesar at
all, not because he did not use crucifixion as a punishment (for
example, in Spain he had three slaves who had been sent out as
spies crucified without further ado, *De Bello Hispaniensi* 20.5; cf.
De Bello Gallico 7.4), but because he did not want to write about
that kind of thing. The same may be true of Lucretius, Virgil,[14]
Statius, the younger Pliny (who as governor in Bithynia must
certainly have condemned offenders to the cross) or Aulus Gellius.
Horace talks of crucifixion only in his *Satires* and *Epistles*; Tacitus,
too, is restrained in talking about crucifixions, at least in the *Annals*,
on the whole mentioning them only as atrocities inflicted by the
Germani or the Britanni on Romans. Others, like Valerius Maximus, the older and younger Senecas, and still more, romance
writers like Petronius and Apuleius, had fewer hesitations here.
The situation is very similar with Greek writers (see pp. 77ff. below). That means, however, that the relative scarcity of references to
crucifixions in antiquity, and their fortuitousness, are less a historical
problem than an aesthetic one, connected with the sociology of
literature. Crucifixion was widespread and frequent, above all in
Roman times, but the cultured literary world wanted to have nothing to do with it, and as a rule kept quiet about it.

[14] The only evidence I have been able to find in Virgil is the uncertain
Priapean poem *Catalepton* 2a.18, where *crux* and cudgel are menacing
thieves (see pp. 66f. n. 2 below).

6

Crucifixion and Roman Citizens

It is usually assumed that there was no question of Roman citizens being executed on the cross, and that the punishment was limited to slaves and *peregrini*. This is only partly correct. There was an archaic, ancient Roman punishment, hanging on the 'barren tree' (*arbor infelix*), which could be imposed even on Romans in cases of serious crime and high treason (*perduellio*). Originally this was probably a way of sacrificing the criminal to the gods of the underworld. According to an old Roman law 'of Romulus' the traitor died 'as a sacrifice for the Zeus of the underworld' (ὡς θῦμα τοῦ κατα-χθονίου Διός, Dionysius of Halicarnassus, *Antiquitates Romanae* 2.10.3). From the third or second century BC this punishment was evidently interpreted as crucifixion.[1] However, with very few exceptions it was hardly ever imposed. When Scipio the Elder crucified deserters who were Roman citizens and had been handed over by the Carthaginians at the end of the Second Punic War, he did so because by their act of high treason they had forfeited the protection

[1] Cf. already T. Mommsen (see bibliography), 919, though in fact he makes too little distinction between the various forms of execution. K. Latte (see bibliography), 1614, does not explain the interpretation of the *arbor infelix* procedure by Cicero as crucifixion. Ovid, *Amores* 1.12, Seneca, *Epistulae morales* 10.1 (*infelix lignum = crux*) and Minucius Felix, *Octavius* 24.7 (*infelix stipes = crux*) are also allusions to the *arbor infelix*. See also C. D. Peddinghaus (see bibliography), 21 and n.139, and C. Brecht, *perduellio*, PW XIX 1, 624f. Servius, *Scholion in Georgica* 1. 501 (Thilo/Hagen III, p.215), says that betrayal of the secret name of the divinity of Rome was punished by crucifixion. The 'hanging up for Ceres' (*suspensumque Cereri necari iubebant*, Pliny the Elder, *Historia Naturalis* 18.3.12) threatened in the Twelve Tables is probably connected with the *arbori infelici suspendere*; T. Mommsen, op. cit., 631f. n.8, sees it as crucifixion, as do P. Garnsey (see bibliography), 128 n. 10, and L. Gernet (see bibliography), 292; K. Latte, op. cit., 1614, differs.

of citizenship.[2] Verres had P. Gavius, who has already been mentioned, crucified in Messina with his gaze towards the mother
country because of the nature of the charge made against him, that
he was a spy of the rebellious slaves of Spartacus who were fighting in
Italy.[3] This legal practice was maintained until the time of the late
empire. The jurist Julius Paulus gives crucifixion (*furca* = gallows,
the word which replaced the 'holy' word cross in legal literature after
Constantine) or burning as the punishment for deserters (*transfugae
ad hostes*) and those who betray secrets (*Digest* 48.19.38.1), and
Modestinus, who is a little later (49.16.3.10) gives torture and
bestiae, or the cross.[4] In having Jews who were Roman knights
(ἄνδρας ἱππικοῦ τάγματος) flogged and crucified in Jerusalem in the critical weeks immediately before the outbreak of the
Jewish War in AD 66, the Roman procurator Gessius Florus, like
Verres, will have been punishing acts of high treason (Josephus,
BJ 2.308). Galba, who had studied the law, when governor in
Spain condemned to crucifixion a guardian who had poisoned his
ward for the sake of the legacy; when the condemned man protested that he was a Roman citizen, Galba had him fastened to a
particularly high cross which was painted white (Suetonius, *Galba*
9.2).[5] Of course, Suetonius concludes from this that Galba was

---

[2] Livy 30.43.13; cf. Valerius Maximus 2.7.12 (see pp. 29f. above). The
war had immeasurably intensified the cruelty employed to maintain
military discipline. One example is the action of Pleminius against two
mutinous officers (204 BC), Diodorus Siculus 27.4.4 and Livy 29.9.10;
29.18.14: *uerberatos seruilibus omnibus suppliciis cruciando occidit, mortuos
deinde prohibuit sepeliri* (having flogged them, he executed them by
torturing them with all the torments applied to slaves (p. 51 n. 1 below)
and then forbade that their bodies should be buried).
[3] Cicero, *In Verrem* 2.5.158ff., 161: *eum speculandi causa in Siciliam a
ducibus fugitivorum esse missum* (sent to Sicily by the leaders of the fugitive
army for spying).
[4] Cf. A. Müller, *Neue Jahrbücher für das klassische Altertum* 17, 1906,
554f.
[5] For the height of the cross as an expression of contempt see Esther
5.14; Artemidorus, *Oneirocriticon*, see below p. 77 n. 24. Pseudo-Manetho,
Apotelesmatica 1.148; 5.219; *Anthologia Graeca* 11.192 (Beckby III, p.
640), of Lucillius; Justin, *Epitome* 18.7.15: Malchus ordered that his son
Cathalus in Carthage *cum ornatu suo in altissimam crucem in conspectu urbis
suffigi* (with his accoutrements should be fastened to a very high cross in the
sight of the city); 22.7.9: Bomilcar *de summa cruce*; Sallust, *Historiae* fr.

excessive in his punishment of criminals (*in coercendis delictis . . . immodicus*). According to the *Historia Augusta*, which is, however, very unreliable historically, various emperors used crucifixion to maintain military discipline in the army, but the use of the *servile supplicium* (see pp. 51ff. below) was denounced as being especially cruel. Celsus, said to be a usurper under Gallienus, who only ruled for seven days, was crucified after his death *in imagine*, to the delight of the people, while his body was devoured by dogs. By the public display of his corpse on a gibbet the dead usurper was exposed to general abuse and mockery.[6]

There is one classic case in which the death penalty was even asked for over a member of the Roman nobility and a senator, with a reference to the old custom of hanging those guilty of high treason on the *arbor infelix*: this was the trial of C. Rabirius in 63 BC, which was instituted by Caesar. The prosecution was made by the tribune T. Labienus, a committed supporter of Caesar, and the defence was led in a masterly way by Cicero. The accused was charged with the murder of a tribune of the people which had taken place thirty-seven years earlier. When Cicero made his plea to the assembly of the people, the danger of crucifixion had already been averted, and

---

3.9 (Maurenbrecher II, p. 113): (in the case of the pirates) *In quis notissimus quisque aut malo dependens verberabatur aut immutilato corpore improbe patibulo eminens affigebatur* (the most notorious were either hung from the mast and flogged or fastened high up on a gibbet without being tortured first). The usual mutilation was not inflicted, since the victim was to suffer a long time. The manuscripts have *improbi*; Kritzius (Sallust, *Opera* III, 1853, 344f.) reads *improbo* with Corte and refers to Plutarch, *Pompey* 24.

[6] *Scriptores Historiae Augustae* 24 (Trebellius Pollio, *Tyranni triginta* 29.4): *imago in crucem sublata persultante vulgo, quasi patibulo ipse Celsus videretur adfixus* (his image was set up on a cross, while the mob pranced around as though they were looking at Celsus himself nailed to a gibbet). The horror story is probably invented, but it does go back to historical examples, see Hohl, *PW* 2.R.VII, 1, 130. In *Scriptores Historiae Augustae* 19 (Iulius Capitolinus, *Maximini* 16.6), the senate acclaims: *inimicus senatus in crucem tollatur . . . inimici senatus vivi exurantur* (let the foe of the senate be crucified . . . let the foes of the senate be burnt alive). According to Herodian 3.8.1 and Dio Cassius (Xiphilin, *Epitome*) 75.7.3, Septimius Severus had the head of his adversary Albinus publicly impaled in Rome (τὴν δὲ κεφαλὴν ἐς τὴν 'Ρώμην πέμψας ἀνεσταύρωσεν), cf. below p. 60.

the only risk was exile and the confiscation of property. Nevertheless, in the first section of his speech (*Pro Rabirio* 9–17) Cicero once again described in detail, in a rhetorical *tour de force*, the penalty with which Rabirius had been threatened. By referring to it he sought to show that the prosecutor, far from being a friend of the people (*popularis*), would be quite the opposite, if he wanted to restore the barbarous customs and the tyranny of the period of the monarchy. Since H.-W. Kuhn has given a wrong interpretation of the decisive sentence in this speech, which is often quoted, and in his recent investigation has drawn misleading consequences from it, I must go into the matter in more detail.[7] I shall therefore quote the whole paragraph which includes the sentence in question:

Misera est ignominia iudiciorum publicorum, misera multatio bonorum, miserum exsilium; sed tamen in omni calamitate retinetur aliquod vestigium libertatis. Mors denique si proponitur, in libertate moriamur, carnifex vero et obductio capitis et nomen ipsum crucis absit non modo a corpore civium Romanorum sed etiam a cogitatione, oculis, auribus. *Harum enim omnium rerum non solum eventus atque perpessio sed etiam condicio, exspectatio, mentio ipsa denique indigna cive Romano atque homine libero est* (ch. 16).

(How grievous a thing it is to be disgraced by a public court; how grievous to suffer a fine, how grievous to suffer banishment; and yet in the midst of any such disaster we retain some degree of liberty. Even if we are threatened with death, we may die free men. *But the executioner, the veiling of the head and the very word 'cross' should be far removed not only from the person of a Roman citizen but from his thoughts, his eyes and his ears.* For it is not only the actual occurrence of these things or the endurance of them, but liability to them, the expectation, indeed the very mention of them, that is unworthy of a Roman citizen and a free man.)

As in the second oration against Verres, where the crucifixion of a Roman citizen is put at the end as a rhetorical climax, with these sentences the first main part of the speech for the defence

----

[7] H.-W. Kuhn (see bibliography), 8: 'This saying of Cicero which is so favoured by theologians (albeit in an abbreviated form) is hardly suitable for giving a characteristic contemporary example of the understanding of crucifixion common at the time.' Kuhn himself has 'abbreviated' the Cicero text very considerably, not to say falsified it, and he has not verified his conclusions by the ancient sources.

reaches its peak.[8] The mere fact that C. Rabirius is being tried publicly is an evil, not to mention that he is threatened with the confiscation of his property and banishment. But even in the case of the death penalty against a Roman citizen, the victim is left some freedom if he is allowed to choose for himself the way in which he is to die. This was certainly not the case in the inflicting of the archaic, barbarous punishment of the *arbori infelici suspendere*, which was worthy of a Tarquinius Superbus (*Tarquini, superbissimi atque crudelissimi regis*).[9] He devised those songs of the torture chamber (*ista . . . cruciatus carmina*), which Labienus, 'the people's friend', had dug up again (ch. 13). Here Cicero is referring to the ancient formula of execution, the most important part of which he quotes himself:

I, lictor, conliga manus, caput obnubito, arbori infelici suspendito.[10]

[8] For Cicero's speech and the trial see the introduction to the German translation by M. Fuhrmann, *Marcus Tullius Cicero, Sämtliche Reden* II, 1970, 197ff.; J. van Ooteghem, 'Pour une lecture candide du *Pro C. Rabirio*', *Études classiques* 32, 1964, 234–46; C. Brecht, op. cit. (p. 39 n. 1), 634f.; K. Büchner, 'M. Tullius Cicero', *PW* 2. R. VII 1, 870ff. The trial took place shortly before Cicero's struggle with Catiline over the consulate and the Catiline conspiracy. The situation in Rome was very tense.

[9] Pliny the Elder, *Historia Naturalis* 36.107: Tarquinius Superbus (not Priscus) had all suicides hung on the cross: *omnium ita defunctorum corpora figeret cruci spectanda civibus simul et feris volucribusque laceranda* (fastened the bodies of all who had died in this way to the cross to be seen by the citizens and to be torn by wild beasts and birds). The shamefulness of crucifixion – even if only of a corpse – becomes particularly clear in this quotation. Cf. also Livy 1.49; Lydus, *De mensibus* 29 (Wünsch, p. 87).

[10] At more length in the account of the trial of the Horatii in Livy 1.26.6f.; cf. 11. According to him the old formula ran: *duumviri perduellionem iudicent; si a duumviris provocarit, provocatione certato; si vincent, caput obnubito; infelici arbori reste suspendito; verberato vel intra pomerium vel extra pomerium* (let the duumvirs pronounce him guilty of treason; if he shall appeal from the duumvirs, let the appeal be heard; if they win, let the lictor veil his head, let him bind him with rope to a barren tree, let him scourge him either inside or outside the *pomerium*). The proceedings were introduced by the command of one of the *duumviri*: *Publi Horati, tibi perduellionem iudico . . . i, lictor, colliga manus.* Livy does not speak of the *crux*: (10) *eum sub furca vinctum inter verbera et cruciatus videre potestis?* but knows of the horrific nature of the punishment: (11) *a tanta foeditate supplicii*; i.e. here the victim is flogged to death; see M. Fuhrmann, 'Verbera', *PW* Suppl. IX, (1589–97) 1591.

(Lictor, go bind his hands, veil his head, hang him on the tree of shame!)

The three terms quoted at the climax of the speech are not, as Kuhn thinks, any three despised forms of execution, including '*inter alia*' the cross, 'but also the worthless covering of the head'.[11] What we have here is a description of the terrible process of the *arbori infelici suspendere*, i.e. crucifixion, following the legal practice of the time: the executioner ties the criminal's hands, covers his head and hangs him on the cross. In any case, Cicero makes a clear distinction between *carnifex*, *obductio capitis* and the real punishment, the *crux*; only the very name (*nomen ipsum*) of the latter is intolerable for a Roman citizen. The translation chosen by Kuhn, 'the very word cross',[12] illustrates this accentuation clearly. Kuhn's view that what we have here is merely 'the aesthetic judgment of a man with the rank of an *eques*, who stood well apart from the greater mass of the people, even from Roman citizens', represents a complete disregard of historical reality. Cicero was not speaking before the senate, but before the *consilium plebis*,[13] and the whole of his speech for the defence was formulated with a view to its effect on the people. And he was successful. C. Rabirius was acquitted. The passage which immediately follows this one shows that Cicero was skilfully playing on the fears of the common man. On being freed (*manumissio*), even Roman slaves are liberated by the touch of the praetor's staff 'from the fear of all these torments'. There follows an argument *a minori ad maius*: 'Are neither acts (of history), age nor your honours (of citizenship) to protect a man from flogging, from the executioner's hook and finally from the terror of the cross (*a crucis denique terrore*)?'[14] Thus, like the documentation from the second oration against Verres, Cicero's speech *Pro Rabirio* must be seen as important ancient evidence for the horror and disgust felt at crucifixion. In no way can I Corinthians 1.26, 'not many

[11] H.-W. Kuhn, loc. cit.

[12] Ibid., cf. the very similar translation by M. Fuhrmann, op. cit. (n. 91), 209: 'and the mere designation "cross"'.

[13] K. Büchner, op. cit. (p. 43 n. 8 above), 871; this already follows from the address *Quirites*.

[14] *Pro Rabirio* 16; cf. Livy 22.13.9: *et ad reliquorum terrorem in cruce sublato.*

were powerful, not many were of noble birth . . .', a passage which has been so misused, be applied in the opposite sense. Even if the Christians in Corinth, a Roman colony founded by freedmen, were predominantly simple citizens (but cf. Rom. 16.23: Erastus, the city treasurer), they must have found crucifixion quite as horrific a punishment as did the simple citizens of Roman cities, freedmen and slaves at the time of the Civil War.

7

Crucifixion as a Penalty for Rebellious Foreigners, Violent Criminals and Robbers

Crucifixion was already, as in Rome, the punishment for serious crimes against the state and for high treason among the Persians, to some degree in Greece and above all among the Carthaginians. That is, it was a religious-political punishment, with the emphasis falling on the political side; however, the two aspects cannot yet be separated in the ancient world. It was a source of wonder to the Romans that the Carthaginians (unlike the Romans themselves) tended to crucify especially generals and admirals who had either been defeated or who proved too wilful.[1] Crucifixion was also a means of waging war and securing peace, of wearing down rebellious cities under siege, of breaking the will of conquered peoples[2] and of bringing mutinous troops or unruly provinces under control. In contrast to the Carthaginians, the Romans as a rule spared their own nobility and Roman citizens, but otherwise their practice was the same. And we must ask whether at the main crises of the Civil War the threat of crucifixion did not sometimes become a reality.[3]

[1] Polybius 1.11.5; 1.24.6; 1.74.9 etc.; Livy 38.48.12: *ubi in crucem tolli imperatores dicuntur* (where generals are said to be crucified); cf. Valerius Maximus 2.7 ext. 1; Justin, *Epitome* 18.7.15; Livy 28.37.2.

[2] Crucifixions at the sacking or siege of cities: see p. 22 n.1: Babylon; pp.69f.: Barca in Cyrenaica; p.73: Tyre (by Alexander); pp.25f. n.17: Jerusalem (by Titus and Varus). The fortress of Machaerus was forced into surrender in exchange for safe conduct by the threat of crucifying a prisoner, p.8.

[3] See Cicero, *Philippicae* 13.21 against Marcus Antonius: *hostis taeterrimus omnibus bonis cruces ac tormenta minitatur* (a most hideous enemy is threatening all good men with crucifixion and torture); Lucan, *De Bello Civili* 7.303f.: Caesar's speech before Pharsalus:

Josephus gives us numerous instances from Judaea (see above, p. 26 n. 17) that it was used excessively to 'pacify' rebellious provincials; the same thing may also have happened in other unruly provinces, though ancient historians tended to pass over such 'trifling matters' in silence.[4] Strabo (3.4.18 = C 165) reports that the wild, freedom-loving Cantabrians in northern Spain continued to sing their songs of victory even when they were nailed to the cross.[5] According to Roman law, rebellious subjects were not 'enemies' (*hostes*), but common 'bandits' (*latrones*, or, as Josephus tends to call the Jewish rebels after the capture of Jerusalem,

---

Aut merces hodie bellorum aut poena parata.
Caesareas spectate cruces, spectate catenas
Et caput hoc positum rostris effusaque membra.

(Today either the reward or the penalty of war is before us. Picture to yourself the crosses and the chains in store for Caesar, my head stuck upon the rostrum and my bones unburied.)

See also Dio Cassius 30–35, fr. 109.4; Valerius Maximus 9.2.3 and Appian, *Bella Civilia* 4.20, for the impalement of the corpses of opponents in the Civil War. Cf. A. W. Lintott (see bibliography), 35ff.

[4] Seneca, *Dialogue* 4 (*De ira* 2) 5.5, gives as an example the fact that in the province of Asia (AD 11/12) the proconsul Volesus had three hundred men executed by the axe in one day, and in full awareness of his *imperium* exclaimed (in Greek): *O rem regiam.* The only other thing that we know about him is that he was later put on trial by the senate for atrocities; we only hear of what he did from Seneca, quite by chance. What would we know about the crucifixions in Palestine without Josephus? Tacitus, *Histories* 5.8–13, does not say a word about them. People tended to be as silent in those days about their own atrocities as dictators and their willing journalists are now.

[5] Cf. Josephus, *BJ* 3.321, about a Jew who was crucified before Jotapata and laughed at the death on the cross devised by his torturers, and 2.153 (the Essenes) and 7.418 (the Sicarii in Egypt); Seneca, *Dialogue* 7 (*De vita beata*) 19.3: . . . *nisi quidam ex patibulo suos spectatores conspuerent* (did not some of them spit upon spectators from their own crosses); Silius Italicus, *Punica* 1. 179ff., the description of a Spanish slave who wanted to be crucified with his master:

superat ridetque dolores,
spectanti similis, fessosque labore ministros
increpitat dominique crucem clamore reposcit.

(He was the master still and despised the suffering; like a mere onlooker he blamed the torturer's assistants for flagging in their task and loudly demanded to be crucified like his master.)

λῃσταί). For them the characteristic death penalty was either crucifixion or being thrown to the wild beasts (*bestiis obici*).[6] We find evidence for this not so much among historians and orators as in the romance (then, as now, people lived on a diet of crime, sex and religion), the popular fable and in astrological and late Roman legal sources. An essential part of the action of the *Novelle* about the matron of Ephesus inserted into Petronius' *Satyricon* is the crucifixion of a group of robbers who are watched over by a soldier so that relatives do not come and steal the bodies:

> When the governor of the province ordered the robbers to be fastened to crosses ...
>
> (*cum interim imperator provinciae latrones iussit crucibus affigi*, 111.5).[7]

The *Metamorphoses* of Apuleius and in the same way the Greek romances treat the profitable theme of 'robbers and crucifixion' in great detail.[8] In the view of various Roman jurists, notorious robbers (*famosi latrones*) should be crucified if possible at the scene of their misdeeds (*Digest* 48.19.28.15).[9] In the astrological literature

[6] M. Hengel, *Die Zeloten*, 31ff.; cf. also R. MacMullen, *Enemies of the Roman Order*, Cambridge, Mass. 1966, 192ff., 255ff., 350ff. According to Dio Cassius 62.11.3f., Paulinus said before the battle against the British leader Boudicca that the Romans were not fighting against enemies of equal status, but against their slaves. The Romans also looked upon Syrians and Jews in a similar way, see M. Hengel, *Juden, Griechen und Barbaren*, SBS 76, 1976, 78f.

[7] Cf. Phaedrus, *Fabulae Aesopi, Appendix Perottina* 15 (Guaglianone, pp. 101ff.).

[8] The robber theme runs right through Apuleius' romance. The crucifixion theme appears in 1.14.2; 1.15.4; 3.17.4; 4.10.4; 'fatally fettering him to the tree of torment' (see the translation by R. Helm); 6.31.2; 6.32.1; 10.12.3; cf. also 8.22.4f. 3.9.1f. is typical: *Nec mora, cum ritu Graeciensi ignis et rota, cum omne flagrorum genus inferuntur. Augetur oppido, immo duplicatur mihi maestitia, quod integro saltim mori non licuerit. Sed anus illa ... : 'Prius,' inquit, 'optimi cives, quam latronem istum, miserorum pignorum meorum peremptorem cruci adfigatis ...'* (And there was no long delay, for according to the custom of Greece, the fire, the wheel and many other torments were brought in; then straightway my sadness increased, or rather was duplicated, because I would not be allowed to die with whole members. But the old woman said, 'Before you fasten this thief who has destroyed my wretched children to the cross ...').

[9] Cf. also *Collectio legum Mosaicarum et Romanarum* 1.6 (T. Mommsen, *Collectio librorum iuris anteiustiniani* III, p. 138), and M. Hengel, *Die Zeloten*, 33f.

and the ancient treatises on dreams it almost goes without saying that the just fate of the robber is to die on the cross.[10] The imposition of the penalty of crucifixion upon robbers and rebels in the provinces was under the free jurisdiction of the local governor, based on his *imperium* and the right of *coercitio* to maintain peace and order.[11] Roman provincial administration had no separation between the authority of the army and the police and legal power. In the imperial provinces the governors were also in command of troops; carrying out sentences on rebels and men of violence had a marked military character. The 'robbers' or 'pirates' also, of course, took revenge by sometimes inflicting crucifixion on their victims.[12] As a rule the rural population were grateful when a governor took a hard line against the plague of robbers, which was widespread and from which they suffered severely. And since, under the *Pax Romana* of the first century, times were peaceful, law was relatively secure and the administration functioned well,[13] crucifixion was an

[10] Firmicus Maternus, *Mathesis* 8.22.3, on those born in the seventh segment of Cancer: *quodsi Lunam et horoscopum Mars radiatione aliqua aspexerit, latrocinantes crudeli feritate grassantur. Sed hi aut in crucem tolluntur, aut publica animadversione peribunt* (But if the moon and Mars are both in aspect to the ascendant, robbers act with cruel ferocity. But these will either be crucified or will perish by some public punishment.) Cf. *Catalogus Codicum Astrologorum Graecorum* VIII, 1, 1929, p. 176 lines 13–17. For Pseudo-Manetho see above, p. 9; for Artemidorus' treatise on dreams see pp. 8f. above and 77 below.

[11] For the crucifixion of 'highwaymen' and 'robbers' see e.g. also Chariton 3.4.18; Aesop, *Fabulae* 157, lines 6f. (Hausrath I, p. 184); Phaedrus, *Fabulae Aesopi* 3.5.10; pirates (see pp. 79f.): Hyginus, *Fabulae* 194. Most instances are provided by Josephus, see above pp. 25f., and *Antiquitates* 20.102. According to a version of the romance of Alexander, which was written at the end of the third century AD, Darius threatened Alexander in a letter that he would have him crucified like a common robber chief or as a 'renegade': *Vita Alexandri* cod. L 1.36.5 (van Thiel, p. 54).

[12] Sallust, *Historiae* fr. 3.9 (see p. 40 n. 5 above); Ps. Quintilian, *Declamationes* 5.16 (Lehnert, p. 103); Seneca the Elder, *Controversiae* 7.4.5; Apuleius, *Metamorphoses* 6.31f.; Xenophon, *Ephesiaca* 4.6.2.

[13] There is a background in reality to the well-known homage paid by the sailors of Alexandria to Augustus, Suetonius, *Augustus* 98.2: *per illum se vivere, per illum navigare, libertate atque fortunis per illum frui* ('by him they lived, by him they sailed and by him they enjoyed liberty and good fortune'). The Mediterranean was now free of pirates. In a similar way Augustus purged Italy of highwaymen: Appian, *Bella Civilia* 5.132.

instrument to protect the populace against dangerous criminals and violent men, and accordingly brought contempt on those who suffered it. Because the robbers often drew their recruits from runaway slaves, abhorrence of the criminal was often combined here with disgust at the punishment meted out to slaves. Semi-barbarian and more disturbed areas were an exception here, and refractory and unsettled Judaea was a special case. In the eyes of the average Roman citizen and even of the diaspora Jews the 'dangers from robbers' (κίνδυνοι λῃστῶν II Corinthians 11.26) had a positive connection with the need for a magistrate to wield the sword, who is mentioned in Romans 13.4. The sight of crucified robbers served as a deterrent and at the same time exacted some satisfaction for the victim:

> *ut et conspectu deterreantur alii ab isdem facinoribus et solacio sit cognatis et adfinibus interemptorum eodem loco poena reddita, in quo latrones homicidia fecissent (Digest 48.19.28.15).*

> (That the sight may deter others from such crimes and be a comfort to the relatives and neighbours of those whom they have killed, the penalty is to be exacted in the place where the robbers did their murders.)

Quintilian could therefore praise the crucifixion of criminals as a good work: in his view the crosses ought to be set up on the busiest roads.[14]

---

[14] *Declamationes* 274 (Ritter, p.124): *quotiens noxios crucifigimus celeberrimae eliguntur viae, ubi plurimi intueri, plurimi commoveri hoc metu possint. omnis enim poena non tam ad (vin)dictam pertinet, quam ad exemplum.* (Whenever we crucify the guilty, the most crowded roads are chosen, where the most people can see and be moved by this fear. For penalties relate not so much to retribution as to their exemplary effect.) For crucifixion at the scene of the crime see also Chariton 3.4.18; Justin, *Epitome* 22.7.8; cf. Alexander Severus, below p.60.

8

The 'Slaves' Punishment'

In most Roman writers crucifixion appears as the typical punishment for slaves. One might almost say that this was a Roman peculiarity, in contrast to what we know about crucifixion among the Persians, Carthaginians and other peoples. In his second speech against Verres Cicero speaks with rhetorical exuberance of the supreme and ultimate penalty for slaves (*servitutis extremum summumque supplicium*, 5.169, cf. p. 33 n. 1 above). The term 'slaves' punishment' (*servile supplicium*) appears in Valerius Maximus, a contemporary of Tiberius, in Tacitus, in two authors of the *Historia Augusta* and for cruel torturing to death in Livy.[1] How-

---

1 Valerius Maximus 2.7.12 on the crucifixion of Roman deserters by Scipio Africanus maior in Africa: *non prosequar hoc factum ulterius, et quia Scipionis est et quia Romano sanguini quamuis merito perpesso seruile supplicium insultare non adtinet* (I will not pursue this matter further, both because it concerns Scipio and because Roman blood should not be insulted by paying the slaves' penalty, however deservedly); Tacitus, *Histories* 4.11 (see pp. 59ff. below); cf. 2.72: *sumptum de eo supplicium in servilem modum* (suffered the punishment usually inflicted on slaves); *Scriptores Historiae Augustae* 15 (Iulius Capitolinus, *Macrinus*) 12.2: *nam et in crucem milites tulit et servilibus suppliciis semper adfecit* (for he even crucified soldiers and always imposed the punishments meted out to slaves); *Scriptores Historiae Augustae* 6 (Vulcacius Gallicanus, *Avidius Cassius*) 4.6: . . . *rapi eos iussit et in crucem tolli servilique supplicio adfici, quod exemplum non extabat* (he had them arrested and crucified and punished them with the punishment of slaves, for which there was no precedent). Cf. also Horace, *Satires* I.8.32: *servilibus . . . peritura modis*. Livy 29.18.14 uses the formula in connection with executions by Pleminius during the Second Punic War in 204 BC: *dein uerberatos seruilibus omnibus suppliciis cruciando occidit, mortuos deinde prohibuit sepeliri* (having flogged them, he executed them by torturing them with all the torments applied to slaves and then forbade that their bodies should be buried); cf. 29.9.10: *laceratosque omnibus quae pati corpus ullum potest suppliciis interfecit nec satiatus vivorum poena insepultos proiecit* (when they had been mangled by every

ever, the matter is to be found portrayed in the crudest terms in
Plautus (*c.* 250 to 184 BC). He is also the first writer, so far as we
know, to give evidence of Roman crucifixions. At the same time,
this poet who presents the world of Roman slaves in an inimitable
way, describes crucifixion more vividly and in greater detail than
any other Latin writer.[2] The antiquity and frequency of the
institution is evident from the much-quoted confession of Sceledrus
in the *Miles Gloriosus*, which was probably written about 205 BC:

> I know the cross will be my grave: that is where my ancestors are, my
> father, grandfathers, great-grandfathers, great-great-grandfathers.
>
> (*scio crucem futuram mihi sepulcrum;*
> *ibi mei maiores sunt siti, pater, auos, proauos, abauos,* 372f.)

For Plautus, slaves have been executed on the cross 'from time im-
memorial'. The deceitful slave Chrysalus is afraid that when his
master returns and finds out about his frauds he will certainly
change his name: '*facietque extemplo Crucisalum me ex Chrysalo*
(he will immediately change me from Chrysalus to Crucisalus,
Bacchides 362), i.e. instead of a 'gold-bearer' he will be a 'cross-
bearer'; that is, he will have to drag his cross to the place of
execution. The slave must always reckon with this cruel death, and
he counters this threat in part with grim 'gallows-humour'.[3]

---

torment which a human body can endure, he put them to death and, not
satisfied with the penalty paid by the living, he cast them out unburied).
The extreme cruelty and shamefulness of the penalty is stressed here.

[2] See G. E. Duckworth, *The Nature of Roman Comedy*, Princeton 1952,
288ff.: 'Master and Slave'. For the dating of Plautus' writings see Sonnen-
burg, 'T. Maccius Plautus', *PW* XIV, 95ff.

[3] Deceit practised by slaves and their punishment in Plautus really re-
quires a monograph to itself. I can only give a few references here: see also
p. 7 n. 13. Cf. *Asinaria* 548ff. (the victory of deceit over all punishment);
Miles gloriosus 539f.; *Mostellaria* 1133; *Persa* 855f.; *Mostellaria* 359ff.: the
slave Tranio,

> *Ego dabo ei talentum primus qui in crucem excucurrerit;*
> *sed ea lege, ut offigantur bis pedes, bis bracchia.*
> *Ubi id erit factum, a me argentum petito praesentarium.*

> (I'll give a talent to the first man to charge my cross and take it on con-
> dition that his legs and arms are double-nailed. When this is attended
> to he can claim the money from me cash down.)

Terence uses the topic of the cross in a much more restrained way, but that may be because he himself had been a slave and did not find it a laughing matter. Since Plautus already takes it for granted that crucifixion is a punishment which has been carried out for ages, both publicly and privately, it cannot first have come to Rome following the First Punic War (264–241 BC). Cicero remarks (*In Verrem* II.5.12) that slaves suspected of rebellion were handed over for crucifixion *more maiorum*. How far the reports of Dionysius of Halicarnassus about the crucifixion of rebellious slaves, which point back towards an earlier period, are historical, remains doubtful; at all events, the historian has depicted the execution of slaves entirely in terms of his own time.[4] According to Livy (22.33.2), in the year 217 BC, the year of the defeat at Lake Trasimene, twenty-five slaves made a conspiracy on the Campus Martius; they were crucified, and the informer received his freedom and 20,000 sesterces. In 196 BC the *praetor peregrinus* M. Acilius Glabrio put down a slave revolt in Etruria with the help of a legion; the *principes*

Stichus 625ff.: Epignomus on the parasite Gelasimus:

> ... *di inmortales! hicquidem pol summam in crucem*
> *cena aut prandio perduci potest!*
> The latter replies: *ita ingenium meumst:*
> *quicumuis depugno multo facilius quam cum fame.*

('Ye immortal gods – what a man! I do believe a dinner or a lunch would induce him to take the highest place at a crucifixion.' 'This is how I'm constituted: there is nothing I find so hard to fight as hunger.')

Cf. Terence, *Andria* 621: Pamphilus: *quid meritu's?* Davos: *crucem* ('What do you deserve?' 'The cross').

[4] *Antiquitates Romanae* 5.51.3; 7.69.1, cf. C. D. Peddinghaus (see bibliography), 24f. See also p. 43 n. 9 on Tarquinius Superbus. Peddinghaus is quite right in stressing that 'there is no definite proof' that crucifixion was introduced via Carthage (25). As Plautus was living and writing as early as the time of the Second Punic War, its significance as a punishment for slaves must be earlier than the Punic Wars, which Peddinghaus gives as a *terminus a quo*. Of course, legendary connections between Rome and Carthage go right back to the sixth century BC. The first trade treaty is said to have been concluded between the two city-states in the year 509 (Polybius 3.23). On the other hand, among the Carthaginians crucifixion was not so markedly a punishment almost exclusively meted out on slaves; it was often inflicted on citizens in cases of high treason.

coniurationis were crucified, and the rest handed back to their owners for punishment (Livy 33.36.3). These accounts suggest that from the state side, crucifixion was practised above all as a deterrent against trouble among slaves and was to be found principally in contexts where the powers of punishment of an individual householder, the *dominica potestas*, were no longer sufficient.[5] According to Tacitus there was a special place in Rome for the punishment of slaves (*locus servilibus poenis sepositus, Annals* 15.60.1), where no doubt numerous crosses were set up. We learn from *Annals* 2.32.2 that this horrific place was on the Campus Esquilinus, the counterpart of the hill of Golgotha in Jerusalem.[6] As a result, Horace calls the vulture the Esquiline bird (*Esquilinae alites*), and Juvenal describes the grisly way in which it disposes of corpses even in Rome (*Satires* 14.77f.):

> The vulture hurries from dead cattle and dogs and crosses
> (*vultur iumento et canibus crucibusque relictis*)
> to bring some of the carrion to her offspring.

There may have been similar places of execution, with crosses and other instruments of torture, in every large city in the Roman empire, as a deterrent to slaves and all law-breakers, and as a sign of a strict and merciless régime.

The great slave rebellions in Italy during the second century BC were the occasion for the excessive use of crucifixion as the *supplicium servile*; fear of the threat of danger from slaves aroused hate and cruelty.[7] Of course our information about crucifixions is

---

[5] In Rome the *tresviri capitales*, as assistants to the praetor, were responsible for law and order. In this capacity they also supervised executions. They already appear in Plautus, *Amphitruo* 155ff.; *Aulularia* 415ff. and *Asinaria* 131; they were feared by slaves. For them and for the decline of private justice practised by the *paterfamilias* see W. Kunkel, *Untersuchungen zur Entwicklung des römischen Kriminalverfahrens in vorsullanischer Zeit*, AAMz NF 56, 1962, 71ff., 115ff., and A. W. Lintott (see bibliography), 102ff.

[6] See also Varro, *De lingua latina* 5.25; Horace, *Satires* 1.8.14ff.; Tacitus, *Annals* 15.40; Suetonius, *Claudius* 25; cf. Catullus, *Carmina* 108.

[7] See W. L. Westermann, 'Sklaverei', PW Suppl. VI, (894–1068) 980f., who refers to Seneca, *Epistulae morales* 47.5: *totidem hostes esse quot servos* ('as many enemies as slaves'), and 976f., with reference to Livy 21.41.10: *non eo solum animo quo adversus alios hostes soletis pugnare velim, sed cum indignatione quadam atque ira, velut si servos videatis vestros arma repente*

completely fortuitous, since it was easier to write about the atrocities of rebellious slaves than about the suffering of those who were defeated. There was also unrest in Italy during the first slave war in Sicily (139–132 BC); according to a later note by Orosius, 450 slaves were *in crucem acti* (*Historiae* 5.9.4). Florus reports that after the Sicilian revolt had been put down, the remainder of the bandits were punished by fetters, chains and crosses (*reliquias latronum compedibus, catenis, crucibusque, Epitome* 2.7 = 3.19.8). A spotlight is cast on the exceptional cruelty with which larger and smaller slave rebellions were suppressed by the report of Appian that after the final defeat of Spartacus the victor Crassus had six thousand prisoners nailed to the cross on the Via Appia between Capua and Rome (*Bella Civilia* 1.120). Before the battle the slave leader had a Roman prisoner crucified between the armies to warn his followers of their fate if they should be defeated (1.119).[8] When Octavian, later to become Augustus, deposed the former triumvir Lepidus in Sicily in 36 BC, he disbanded the troops of Sextus Pompeius. Contrary to the agreement concluded with Sextus he returned

---

contra vos ferentes (to fight not only with that courage with which you are accustomed to fight against the enemy, but with a kind of resentful rage, as if you saw your slaves suddenly take up arms against you). Cf. also E. M. Štaerman, *Die Blütezeit der Sklavenwirtschaft in der römischen Republik*, Wiesbaden 1969, 238ff., 257ff.

[8] Crucifixions in connection with slave troubles in the second and first centuries BC are also mentioned by Cicero, *In Verrem* II.5.3; similarly Valerius Maximus 6.3.5 and Quintilian, *Institutio oratoria* 4.2.17: the praetor L. Domitius had a shepherd crucified in Sicily after he had killed a boar with a spear, since slaves were prohibited from carrying weapons. Valerius Maximus 2.7.9: L. Calpurnius Piso punished in Sicily a *praefectus equitum* who handed out weapons to slaves: *ut qui cupiditate uitae adducti cruce dignissimis fugitiuis tropaea de se statuere concesserant* . . . (led on by a desire for life they allowed fugitives most worthy of the cross to set up their own trophies). Cf. also C. Clodius Licinus, *Rerum Romanorum Reliquiae* 21 (Peter II, p.78). Dionysius of Halicarnassus, *Antiquitates Romanae* 5.51.3 and 7.69.2, similarly presupposes conditions during the slave wars and transfers them to the early period of Rome. Even Cicero, *Pro rege Deiotaro* 26, does not despise this terminology: *quae crux huic fugitiuo potest satis supplici adferre* (what cross can bring adequate punishment to this fugitive)? Cf. J. Vogt, *Sklaverei* (see bibliography), 49f., 60.

the slaves who had been enlisted to their masters for punishment, and had those without masters crucified (Dio Cassius 49.12.4; cf. Appian, *Bella Civilia* 5.131).⁹ In the account which he gives in the *Monumentum Ancyranum* (ch.25), however, he says only that he gave back 30,000 slaves to their masters *ad supplicium sumendum*. The rigorous application of the *servile supplicium* was a consequence of the panic fear of slave rebellions, particularly in Italy, which was constantly fostered by the accumulation of large masses of slaves in the *latifundia* of Italy during the period of Roman 'imperialism' after the Second Punic War. It is all too understandable that this fear sometimes turned into hate.

The Civil War and its proscriptions involved the slaves in a conflict between loyalty to their masters and loyalty to the political authorities, which promised them 10,000 drachmae, freedom and Roman citizenship for the killing of a proscribed master (Appian, *Bella Civilia* 4.11). In at least one instance, however, the indignation of the people compelled the triumviri to crucify a slave who had handed over his master to the killers (Appian, *Bella Civilia* 4.29).¹⁰ Augustus permitted the slave who had betrayed the conspiracy of Fannius Caepio to be nailed to the cross publicly by the father of the conspirator, after the slave had first carried a notice giving the cause of his death around the Forum (Dio Cassius 54.3.7). We also have similar accounts from the second and third centuries AD. Pertinax, himself the son of a freedman, son-in-law of Marcus Aurelius and the capable successor of Commodus (AD 192), who was murdered all too soon, freed all those who had been

⁹ Dio Cassius 49.12.4; cf. Appian, *Bella Civilia* 5.131 and Orosius, *Historiae* 6.18.33: *sex milia, quorum domini non extabant, in crucem egit* (he crucified six thousand, who had no masters).

¹⁰ A similar occurrence is said already to have taken place under Tarquinus Superbus (see p. 43 n. 9 above), Scholion in Juvenal, *Satires* 8.266f. (Wessner, pp. 152f.): *Vindicius servus, qui indicaverit filios Bruti Tarquinio portas velle reserare. quos pater securi feriit, servum autem ut conservatorem patriae manu misit et ut delatorem dominorum cruci adfigit* (Vindicius is the slave who gave evidence that the sons of Brutus wanted to open the gates to Tarquinius. The former their father killed with the axe: he freed the slave as a saviour of his country and crucified him as an informer.) For the role of slaves in proscriptions see J. Vogt, *Sklaverei* (see bibliography), 86ff.

condemned on the basis of denunciations by slaves and had those informers who were slaves crucified (*Scriptores Historiae Augustae* 8: Iulius Capitolinus, *Pertinax* 9.10). The same thing happened again when Macrinus became emperor in AD 217 after the murder of Caracalla. He, too, had all the slaves who had denounced their masters under his cruel predecessor crucified (Herodian 5.2.2). The conflict between the orders of a master and the commands of the state, both of which threatened the slave with crucifixion, or between the goodness of a master and the limitations of class, of which crucifixion was a symbol, became a favourite theme of rhetorical declamation.[11]

Slaves thus had relatively little protection against the whim of their masters and therefore against unjust imposition of the *servile supplicium*. The dialogue between a Roman matron and her husband, given by Juvenal (6.219ff.), says more here than many examples:

'"Crucify that slave", says the wife. "But what crime worthy of death has he committed?", asks the husband. "Where are the witnesses? Who informed against him? Give him a hearing at least. No delay can be too long when a man's life is at stake." "What a fool you are!

[11] Cf. e.g. Seneca the Elder, *Controversiae*, exc. 3.9: *crux servi venenum domino negantis* (the crucifixion of a slave who refuses to give his master poison); Ps. Quintilian, *Declamationes* 380: *crux scripta servo non danti venenum*. Both deal with the popular rhetorical theme of the slave who refuses to give his seriously ill master poison to put him out of his misery in order not to be guilty of poisoning under the *lex Cornelia de sicariis et veneficis*, and thus not to be freed in his testament, but handed over to be crucified. The slave apeals to the tribune, i.e. to the imperial court. Seneca the Elder, *Controversiae* 7.6, records another horror story which deals with mixed marriage between freed slaves and freeborn members of the upper class, which was taboo: a master sets his slave free as a reward for his faithfulness and marries him to his daughter, whereas the other slaves in the city are crucified. He is accused of degrading his daughter to the level of being related to *cruciarii: Si voles invenire generi tui propinquos, ad crucem eundum est* ('If you want to find your son-in-law's relatives', go to the cross', cf. Plautus, *Miles Gloriosus* 372f., see p. 52 above). Servius, *Commentary on Virgil, Aeneid* 3.551 (Thilo/Hagen I, p.436), reports that after their war against Messene the Spartans put an abrupt end to the illegal relationships between Spartan women and slaves and their off-spring: *servos patibulis suffixerunt, filios strangulavere* ('they crucified the slaves and strangled the children'). Here the Roman abhorrence against such liaisons was introduced into Greek history.

Do you call a slave a man? Do you say he has done no wrong? This
is my will and my command: take it as authority for the deed." '

('*Pone crucem servo!' – 'Meruit quo crimine servus*
supplicium? quis testis adest? quis detulit? audi;
nulla umquam de morte hominis cunctatio longa est.'
'*O demens, ita servus homo est? nil fecerit esto;*
Hoc volo, sic iubeo, sit pro ratione voluntas!')[12]

In his defence of A. Cluentius, Cicero accuses the mother of the
accused of having had a slave crucified and at the same time of having had his tongue cut out, so that he could not give evidence (*Pro
Cluentio* 187). In his speech *Pro Milone* he castigates the extraction
of false testimony from slaves in the time of violent faction-fighting
between the *populares* and the *optimates* (ch. 60). If the slave in-
criminated Clodius, the corrupt faction leader of the *populares*,
against his enemy Milo, he faced the cross (*certa crux*); if he
exonerated him, the liberty he hoped for (*sperata libertas*). The men
of old (*maiores*) had rejected testimony by slaves against their
masters in principle.

Of course there was also criticism of excesses of this kind. For
Horace, a master who has his slave crucified because he sur-
reptitiously tasted some fish soup while bringing it in, 'is quite
mad by any reasonable standard'.[13] This attitude was matched by
Augustus' tendency to curb the whims of slave-owners in favour

[12] Seneca the Elder, *Controversiae* 10.5, deals with the case of an Athenian painter who bought an old prisoner of war from Olynthus as a slave
and tortured him to death as the model for a portrait of Prometheus (see
above, pp. 11f.). While the Greek orators utterly condemned the painter, he
was to some extent defended by the Latin ones. Fulda (see bibliography),
56, gives a mediaeval instance of a crucifixion as a model for a painting.

[13] *Satires* 1.3.8ff.: Lucian, *Prometheus* 10 (directed against Zeus): no
one crucifies his cook if he tastes the food. In Horace, *Satires* 2.7.47, a slave
remonstrating with his master says, *peccat uter nostrum cruce dignius*
(which of us commits a sin more worthy of the cross)? In *Epistles* 1.16.46–
48 Horace reports a conversation with his slave:

'*nec furtum feci nec fugi*' *si mihi dicit*
servus, '*habes pretium, loris non ureris,*' *aio.*
'*non hominem occidi.*' '*non pasces in cruce corvos.*'

(If a slave were to say to me, 'I never stole nor ran away', my reply
would be, 'You have your reward, you are not flogged.' 'I never killed
anyone.' 'You will not feed the crows on the cross.')

of the authority of the state. Seneca even went so far as to remark with some degree of satisfaction 'that the cruelty of private slave owners was avenged even by the hands of slaves, who stood under the certain threat of crucifixion' (*sub certo crucis periculo, De Clementia* 1.26.1).

On the other hand, state justice against slaves continued to be harsh, and indeed in the time of the empire freedmen and *peregrini* were increasingly punished with crucifixion in the same way as slaves. Valerius Maximus reports that – still during the Republic – a slave denied having murdered an *equus* although he was tortured six times; finally, however, he confessed and was crucified; another is said to have been condemned although he kept silent while being tortured eight times (8.4.2f.). The 'old custom' of executing (often by crucifixion) all the slaves in a household if the master was murdered was revived in the time of Nero by a decree of the senate (Tacitus, *Annals* 13.32.1), and a few years later it was in fact put into force after the murder of a city prefect, despite the threat of rebellion among the people (14.42–45). The main argument was that the great mass of slaves in Rome could not be kept in check without fear (*non sine metu*, 14.44.3). In the *acta urbis* which Trimalchio suddenly has read out by his *actuarius* during the famous feast, a notice appears between information about property and the selling of cattle and corn: 'The slave Mithridates was crucified for having damned the soul of our Gaius (= Caligula)' (Petronius, *Satyricon* 53.3).[14] It is still the case in the *Sententiae* of the jurist Paulus (5.21.3f.) that the death penalty is threatened not only on all those who ask questions of astrologers about the emperor's future and that of the state, but also on the slave who asks the same question about his master's fate: *Summo supplicio, id est cruce, adficiuntur* (they will meet the most severe punishment, the cross). Imperial slaves and freedmen, who could even rise to the

14 C. D. Peddinghaus (see bibliography), 30, interprets the passage quite nonsensically in terms of an impalement by king Mithridates. For the soul of Gaius see Suetonius, *Caligula* 27.3, and Minucius Felix, *Octavius* 29.5: *et est eis tutius per Iovis genium peierare quam regis* (safer for them to swear falsely by the soul of Jupiter than by the soul of the king). For the whole question cf. Petronius, *Satyricon* 137.2: *si magistratus hoc scierint, ibis in crucem* ('if the magistrates knew this, you would be crucified').

status of an *eques*, were further threatened by the cruelty of individual rulers. Caligula (Suetonius, *Caligula* 12.2) and Domitian (*Domitian* 11.1) are said to have crucified imperial slaves or freedmen at their whim. Vitellius had a treacherous freedman executed *in servilem modum* (Tacitus, *Histories* 2.72.2), and his opponent Vespasian did the same thing with two former slaves whom Vitellius had freed because of their military 'services', honouring them with the status of *eques*. Tacitus reports with satisfaction the execution of the one who had betrayed Tarracina: the fact that the crucified man was fixed to the cross in the insignia of the equestrian order was a general comfort (*solacium* 4.3.2). Of the other, Asiaticus, he records laconically: 'He paid for his hateful power by a slave's punishment' (*malam potentiam servili supplicio expiavit*, 4.11.3). It is said that after the murder of Heliogabalus in AD 222 Alexander Severus not only reduced the imperial slaves and freedmen whom he had promoted to their former state, but if they had been convicted of calumny and bribery, as a deterrent to others he had them crucified 'on the street which his slaves used most frequently on the way to the imperial palace' (*Scriptores Historiae Augustae* 18: Aelius Lampridius, *Alexander Severus* 23.8). The freedmen and women of private individuals were also endangered in the time of the Empire: the freedwoman of a Roman *eques* who, in league with the priests of a temple of Isis in Rome, had helped him to deceive the woman he longed for, was crucified under Tiberius along with the priests of the Egyptian goddess, who were not Roman citizens but only *peregrini*; the temple was pulled down and the effigy of Isis cast into the Tiber. The seducer himself, however, as an *eques*, escaped with banishment because he had acted in the folly of love (Josephus, *Antiquitates* 18.79f.). In other words, even here the class barriers were strictly maintained.[15]

---

[15] Cf. Apuleius, *Metamorphoses* 10.12.3: because of an attempt to murder her stepson, a matron is condemned along with her accomplice, a slave: *novercae quidem perpetuum indicitur exilium, servus vero patibulo suffigitur* (the woman was perpetually exiled and the slave fastened to the gibbet). For the distinction between *honestiores* and *humiliores* cf. also *Anthologia Latina* 794.35:

Crimen opes redimunt, reus est crucis omnis egenus.

(Riches buy off judgment, and the poor are condemned to the cross.)

There was evidently a particularly strong suspicion of religious deception and the illegal practice of 'superstitious foreign cults' (*superstitiones externae*: Tacitus, *Annals* 11.15; cf. 13.32.2) among slaves, freedmen and *peregrini*. This is also a partial explanation of the harsh proceedings in the trials of Christians. We have parallels to this in the persecution of the astrologers (Tacitus, *Annals* 2.32), the Celtic druids (Suetonius, *Claudius* 25; Aurelius Victor, *Caesares* 4.2; cf. Pliny the Elder, *Historia Naturalis* 29.54) and in the punishment of those guilty of the ancient Punic practice of child sacrifice. Christians were also accused of such crimes (Minucius Felix, *Octavius* 9.5). A proconsul of Africa, otherwise unknown, punished with utmost severity the priests of 'Saturn', i.e. the Carthaginian god Baal-Hammon, who kept up this ancient practice of child sacrifice. He had them hanged 'on the very trees of their temple, in the shadow of which they had committed their crimes, as though on consecrated crosses (*votivis crucibus exposuit*).' Tertullian, who hands down this information, refers for it to the eyewitness accounts of the soldiers who performed the execution in the name of the proconsul.[16]

It could, of course, be asked whether for slaves and *peregrini*, who had to reckon with the possibility of crucifixion as a punishment, the cross could be such a deterrent horror as to be a hindrance to the message of the crucified redeemer. The answer is that for these people the horror was even more real and related to personal existence than it was for members of the upper classes. Thus the more capable slaves hoped for freedom, which improved their social and legal situation at least to some extent and gave them the possibility of further social improvement; among the ancient bourgeoisie of the self-made men who had made their way up from the mass of the people, the *libertini* played an important role, as is shown by the example of Trimalchio and the numerous imperial freedmen with some degree of power. An alleged son of god who could not help himself at the time of his deepest need (Mark 15.31),

[16] Tertullian, *Apologeticus* 9.2. For child sacrifice see O. Kaiser, 'Den Erstgeborenen deiner Söhne sollst du mir geben. Erwägungen zum Kinderopfer im Alten Testament', in *Denkender Glaube. Festschrift Carl Heinz Ratschow*, Berlin 1976, 24–48 (for the Carthaginians see 42f. n. 65a), and A. Henrichs, *Die Phoinikika des Lollianos*, 1972, 12ff. (15f.) 32ff.

and who rather required his followers to take up the cross, was hardly an attraction to the lower classes of Roman and Greek society. People were all too aware of what it meant to bear the cross through the city and then to be nailed to it (*patibulum ferat per urbem, deinde offigitur cruci*, Plautus, *Carbonaria*, fr. 2) and feared it; they wanted to get away from it. Moreover, early Christianity was not particularly a religion of slaves; at the time of Paul, and much more so with Pliny and Tertullian, it embraced men of every rank, *omnis ordinis*.[17]

This basic theme of the *supplicium servile* also illuminates the hymn in Philippians 2.6–11. Anyone who was present at the worship of the churches founded by Paul in the course of his mission, in which this hymn was sung, and indeed any reader of Philippians in ancient times, would inevitably have seen a direct connection between the 'emptied himself, taking the form of a slave' (ἑαυτὸν ἐκένωσεν μορφὴν δούλου λαβών) and the disputed end of the first strophe: 'he humbled himself and was obedient unto death, even the death of the cross'. Death on the cross was the penalty for slaves, as everyone knew; as such it symbolized extreme humiliation, shame and torture. Thus the θανάτου δε σταυροῦ is the last bitter consequence of the μορφὴν δούλου λαβών and stands in the most abrupt contrast possible with the beginning of the hymn with its description of the divine essence of the pre-existence of the crucified figure, as with the exaltation surpassing anything that might be conceived (ὁ θεὸς αὐτὸν ὑπερύψωσεν). The one who had died the death of a slave was exalted to be Lord of the whole creation and bearer of the divine name Kyrios. If it did not have θανάτου δὲ σταυροῦ at the end of the first strophe, the hymn would lack its most decisive statement. The careful defence of its unity from both poetical and theological criteria by Otfried Hofius can therefore be supported also from its content, the *supplicium servile*: 'If the climax of the first strophe lies – in terms of both language and content – in the mention of the death of the cross, the assertion that in the pre-Pauline hymn the incarnation was understood as the real saving

---

[17] Pliny the Younger, *Epistulae* 10.96; Tertullian, *Apologeticus* 1.7; *Adversus Nationes* 1.1.2; cf. M. Hengel, *Property and Riches in the Early Church*, ET London and Philadelphia 1975, 36ff. and 64ff.

event and the death merely as its unavoidable consequence can no longer be held to be credible. On the contrary, we are forced to suppose that the hymn already presupposes a firm view of the saving significance of the death of Jesus.'[18]

[18] O. Hofius, *Der Christushymnus Philipper 2,6–11*, WUNT 17, 1976, 17. Cf. 9–17, 56–64. See also M. Hengel, *The Son of God*, 1976, 87f., 91f.

9

The Crucified National Martyr and Metaphorical and Philosophical Terminology

There remains the question whether there is any evidence in the ancient Roman world for a non-Christian, positive interpretation of death by crucifixion, say as the manner of death of a philosopher or a national martyr. After all, the death of such figures was a familiar feature of the ancient world. I have not been able to discover a real historical instance – leaving aside the ambiguous figure of Polycrates (see above, p. 24); however, during the course of tradition the figure of the national hero M. Atilius Regulus was associated with the cross. As an unsuccessful general, Regulus was captured during an expedition to North Africa in the First Punic War. The Carthaginians then sent him back to Rome to arrange the exchange of prisoners or to negotiate a peace treaty with Rome. Once there, however, he counselled the senate to remain firm. Faithful to his promise, given under oath, he is then said to have returned to Carthage, where he was tortured to death by the Carthaginians in revenge. Traditions about the manner of his death vary widely; among those mentioned are slow-working poison, being deprived of sleep, being shut up in a dark room, having his eyelids cut off, being exposed to blinding light and finally also crucifixion, the last-mentioned presumably because it was the form of execution practised in Carthage and was regarded as the *summum supplicium* which embraced all conceivable tortures.

The historical value of this legend, elaborated by Cicero in particular, which would 'do full justice to the imagination of a torturer', is extremely small. 'These unpleasant and historically spurious heroes are a creation of the rhetoric which exercised such an unhealthy influence on Roman historiography after the time of Sulla and of the insipid popular moral philosophy with which we are familiar from Cicero's writings and which was unconscious of its own immorality. They were then celebrated for centuries in declamations composed in prose or poetry.'[1] Above all, Silius Italicus in the second half of the second century AD cannot go far enough in his exaggerated and indeed tasteless reverence for the national martyr:

> I was looking on when Regulus, the hope and pride of Hector's race, was dragged along amid the shouts of the populace to his dark dungeon, with both hands bound fast behind his back; I was looking on when he hung high upon the tree and saw Italy from his lofty cross.
>
> (. . . *vidi, cum robore pendens*
> *Hesperiam cruce sublimis spectaret ab alta, Punica* 2.340–4, cf. 435f.).

Of course, the cross is only one theme among many, and is indeed a latecomer to the scene. In Book 6 a messenger tells Regulus' son Serranus of the bestial cruelty of the Carthaginians (*ritus imitantem irasque ferarum*) and the example given to the whole world by the *veneranda virtus* of his father, who suffered torture joyfully (*placido ore ferentem*). He was deprived of sleep by an instrument of torture.

> That endurance (*patientia*) is greater than all triumphs. His laurels will green throughout the ages, as long as unstained loyalty (*fides*) keeps her seat in heaven and on earth, and will last as long as virtue's name is worshipped (529–50).

It cannot be coincidence that in this last hymn of praise there is no longer any mention of crucifixion.

Seneca sees Regulus in a similar way as a man who proves victorious over all the *terribilia* feared by men: 'Many men have overcome separate trials: Mucius the fire, Regulus the cross, Socrates poison' (*singula vicere iam multi: ignem Mucius, crucem Regulus, venenum Socrates . . ., Epistulae morales* 98.12). He compares him as a proof of faith and patience (*documentum fidei [et] patientiae*) with the effeminate Maecenas (see above, p.30), 'who

[1] See P. v. Rohden, 'Atilius 51', *PW* II, 2086–92 (quotation from 2092). Horace gives the simplest evaluation – without the theme of the cross – in his *Odes* (3.6). Here we simply have *quae sibi barbarus/tortor pararet* (lines 49f.: he knew what the barbarian torturer was preparing for him).

spent as many vigils on a feather bed as he did on the cross' (*tam vigilabis in pluma quam ille in cruce*, Dialogue 1, *De providentia* 3.9f.). Florus stresses that Regulus did not sully his honour either by his voluntary return to Carthage or through extreme suffering, whether in prison or on the cross (*nec ultimo sive carceris seu crucis supplicio deformata maiestas*); rather, and this was much more remarkable, he had become a victor over those who had overcome him, indeed he had even conquered fate (*fortuna*) itself (*Epitome* 1.18 = 2.2.25). Even on the cross, the national martyr is accorded the highest honour which the ancient enlightened world could bestow: he was master of his own destiny. For Tertullian, Regulus was the prototype of the pagan martyr, since – in contrast to the others – 'your Regulus readily initiated the novelty of the cross with its manifold and exquisite cruelty' (*crucis vero novitatem numerosae, abstrusae, Regulus vester libenter dedicauit, Ad Nationes* 1.18.3).

The reason why Regulus was said to have been executed on the cross, contrary to all historical reality, may be found in formulations like that in Cicero, *De Natura Deorum* 3.80: *Cur Poenorum crudelitati Reguli corpus est praebitum* (why the body of Regulus was given over to the cruelty of the Carthaginians). The cross was obviously *par excellence* the expression of this *crudelitas*.

We must also make a brief examination of the *metaphorical* terminology which may also be present, in part, in the Regulus legend. *Crux* could be used as an expression for the utmost torment, even including the pains of love, and sometimes it is difficult to decide whether there is a real reference to the instrument of execution or the death penalty, or whether the language is merely metaphorical. The understanding of crucifixion as the *summum supplicium* surely underlies Columella's remarkable statement, 'the ancients regarded the extreme of the law as the extreme of the cross' (*summum ius antiqui summam putabant crucem, De re rustica* 1.7.2). Cicero describes the mere wish to involve oneself in the tyranny of Caesar as *miserius . . . quam in crucem tolli* (*Ad Atticum* 7.11.2), though this did not prevent him at a later stage from doing just that.[2]

---

[2] Cf. also the comment (*Ad Quintum Fratrem* 1.29) on the *eques* Catienus: *illum crucem sibi ipsum constituere, ex qua tu eum ante detraxisses* (set up for himself a cross from which you had earlier taken him down).

More interest is provided by the few instances where the *summum et servile supplicium* appears in philosophical discussion – in connection with the vivid Cynic and Stoic diatribe. Epictetus thinks that it is wrong to provoke an opponent in a legal dispute, since 'if you want to be crucified, wait, and the cross will come' (if it is to come); the decisive thing is to hearken to the Logos in everything (*Diatribes* 2.2.20).[3] Seneca compares desires (*cupiditates*) with 'crosses into which each one of you drives his own nails' (*cruces, in quos unusquisque uestrum clauos suos ipse adigit*); all hang on their own crosses (*stipitibus singulis pendent*) as though brought to punishment (*ad supplicium acti*). There is an echo of the whole thing in the following sentence, which could fit into a Cynic sermon: they are torn apart by as many desires as crosses (*quot cupiditatibus tot crucibus distrahuntur, Dialogue* 7, *De vita beata* 19.3). Cicero attacks the basic Stoic thesis that pain is not really an evil and that the wise man must be *semper beatus*. His terse counter-argument runs: anyone who is put on a cross cannot be happy (*in crucem qui agitur, beatus esse non potest, De Finibus* 5.84); he cites Polycrates as an example of his thesis (5.92). Like Seneca, Philo uses the image of crucifixion on several occasions to describe the en-slavement of man to his body and the desires which dominate it: souls 'hang on unsouled matter in the same way as those who are crucified are nailed to transitory wood until their death'.[4] The common starting point for these passages is Plato's remark in the *Phaedo* (83cd) that every soul is fastened to the body by desire as though by a nail.[5] The imagery of crucifixion left no room for a

---

Virgil (?), *Catalepton* 2a, 18: *parata namque crux, cave, stat mentula* (be-ware, for the cross is ready and the penis erect). The threat is of the peas-ant's Priapic, phallic cudgel. For the pains of grief, Catullus, *Carmina* 99.4: *suffixum in summa me memini esse cruce* (I remember how I hung impaled on the top of the cross).

[3] In the negative sense, 3.26.22, against those who are stretched out 'like crucified figures' in the baths under the hands of the masseur.

[4] Philo, *De posteritate Caini* 61: ἀψύχων ἐκκρέμανται καὶ καθάπερ οἱ ἀνασκολοπισθέντες ἄχρι θανάτου φθαρταῖς ὕλαις προσήλωνται, cf. *De somniis* 2.213 as interpretation of Gen. 40.19; Prov. 25 with reference to Polycrates (see p. 24 n. 13 above).

[5] Cf. Plutarch, *Moralia* 718D; Iamblichus, quoted in Stobaeus, *Anthologia* 3.5.45 (Wachsmuth/Hense III, p. 270).

positive interpretation, apart from the admonition which was widespread in antiquity, that each man had to bear his own fate; here too the metaphor was one of horror and abomination. It is striking that the metaphorical terminology is limited to the Latin sphere, whereas in the Greek world the cross is never, so far as I can see, used in a metaphorical sense. Presumably the word was too offensive for it to be used as a metaphor by the Greeks.

Crucifixion in the Greek-Speaking World

So far the Greek-speaking world, Greece, Asia Minor, Egypt and Syria, has been deliberately kept at the periphery of our discussion. The sources for crucifixion, which in the period of the empire markedly appears as a Roman punishment, are much fuller in Latin literature than in Greek. However, it would be a mistake to make a distinction in principle between the Latin 'West' and the Greek 'East', or even between the Persian 'East' and the Greek 'West'.[1] Pheretime, the mother of the murdered Arcesilaus, the tyrant of Barca in Cyrenaica, who had those principally involved in the death of her son crucified round the city wall (Herodotus 4.202.1), was as Greek as her victims. Herodotus further shows that even the Athenians could crucify a hated enemy (see pp. 24ff. above); the phrase 'nail to planks', which appears only here, suggests that a real

[1] C. D. Peddinghaus (see bibliography), 9.11f., draws a somewhat un-reliable distinction between 'East' and 'West'; he is followed by E. Brandenburger (see bibliography), 21. It is also wrong to say that 'putting a corpse on show on a stake is evidently a practice found only in the East', as is stated by H.-W. Kuhn (see bibliography), 10 n.33, also following Peddinghaus (see p. 46 n. 3 and Diodorus Siculus 16.61.2; Euripides, *Electra* 896ff.). As well as crucifixion, there is in the East evidence for impalement, with the verbs πηγνύναι, ἀναπείρειν, etc.; Euripides, *Iphigenia in Tauris* 1430; *Rhesus* 513ff.; Diodorus Siculus 33.15.1f.; Dio Cassius 62.7.2; 62.11.4; see also Seneca, *Epistulae morales* 14.5; *Dialogue* 6 (*De consolatione, Ad Marciam*) 20.3; Fulda (see bibliography), 113–16. Plutarch, *Moralia* 499D, the passage cited by Kuhn, ἀλλ' εἰς σταυρὸν καθηλώσεις ἢ σκόλοπι πήξεις, mentions crucifixion and impalement as being presumably the most gruesome forms of execution known to Plutarch, see below p. 77. He cites them in order to illustrate the subsequent anecdote of the fearlessness of the Cyrenaican Theodorus Atheus. The 'East' was no more cruel than the 'West'. For the impalement of the corpse or head of an enemy see p. 24, p. 41 n. 6 and p. 47 n. 3 above.

cross was not used in this case, but the '*tympanum*', which was familiar from their own penal law. This was a flat board made up of
planks (σανίδες) on which criminals were fastened for public display, torture or execution. The seventeen victims discovered in the
well-known find of the tomb at Phaleron from the seventh century
BC were fastened with a ring round their necks and hooks round
their hands and feet. This could be seen as an aggravated form of
ἀποτυμπανισμός, which would come very near to crucifixion if the
victim were nailed down instead of being bound or fastened with
curved nails. Mythological analogies are Ixion, Prometheus (see
above, pp. 11ff.) and Andromeda (see below p. 77).[2] In Aristophanes'
Thesmophoriazusai, Mnesilochus, dressed as a woman, is 'tied to the
plank' for impiety (930, 940); he himself believes that he is doomed
to die and will be a sport and food for the ravens (938, 942, 1029).
He is fastened with nails (1003: ἧλος) which can either be loosened
or driven further in; in this way he 'hangs' on the plank (1027,
1053, 1110) like Andromeda, 'distracted and dying, with throat-
cutting agonies riving him' (1054f.), watched over and taunted by a
Scythian bowman who finally threatens to kill him. The whole
scene may only depict a pillory, but it is not far short of a crucifixion.[3] The report of Duris, the historian and ruler of Samos, that
after the capture of the city Pericles had the ten leaders of the
Samians 'bound to planks' (σανίσι προσδήσας) in the market place
of Miletus, and after they had suffered for ten days gave the order to
beat in their skulls with cudgels, is not as improbable as Plutarch,
who is favourably inclined to the Athenians, suggests (*Pericles*
28.3). This is merely an aggravated form of *apotympanismos*, and

[2] See '*A. Δ. Κεραμόπουλλος* (see bibliography), *passim*. K. Latte (see
bibliography), 1606f., is critical, but he does not do justice to all the arguments put forward by *Κεραμόπουλλος*. The judgment given by I. Barkan
(see bibliography), 63–72, is very balanced, and probably comes closest to
reality. Cf. also J. Vergote (see bibliography), 143, and C. E. Owen, *JTS*
30, 1929, 259–66. τύμπανον could be used to designate the rack, II Macc.
6.19, 28, and the place of scourging (see Vergote, op. cit., 153f.), which indeed could also be carried out on a stake or cross. The inventiveness of the
torturers was greater than words can describe. The connection with
crucifixion is also stressed by L. Gernet (see bibliography), 290ff. and 302ff.
[3] See *Κεραμόπουλλος* op. cit., 27ff.; Barkan, op. cit., 66ff.; Gernet, op.
cit., 304f. Cf. *Suidae Lexicon* s.v. *Κύφωνες*, above p. 25 n. 16.

the most improbable thing is the duration of ten days for the punishment.[4] In Sophocles' Antigone, Creon threatens not merely to kill those who are in the know about the burial of Polyneices but to hang them alive (ζῶντες κρεμαστοί, 308) unless they speak up. According to a fragment of the comedian Cratinus, slaves were often 'tied to planks'.[5] On the other hand, Menander,[6] Alciphron,[7] Antiphanes[8] and Longus[9] speak of 'hanging'. This, however, is probably not in the sense of killing but of scourging. The word probably also has the same significance in a decree of Antiochus XIII Asiaticus (?), who expelled all philosophers from his sphere of rule. The young men who were found in their company were to be 'hanged' (κρεμήσονται, Athenaeus 12, p. 547b). In the *Tarantinoi* of Alexis the hero would like most of all to 'fasten to the wood' or 'impale' the parasite Theodotus (ἀναπήξαιμ' ἐπὶ τοῦ ξύλου, Athenaeus 4, p. 134a). The Ptolemaic papyri know of both 'hanging'[10] and ἀποτυ(μ)πανίζειν; it must remain open whether the latter was done merely for scourging, or in fact for execution.[11] According to

---

[4] See Κεραμόπουλλος, op. cit., 26f., 31; Barkan, op. cit., 64f.; P. Ducrey (see bibliography), 212. J. Vergote, *RAC* VIII, 116f., conjectures a pillory.

[5] Scholion in Aristophanes, *Thesmophoriazusai* 940 = fr. 341 (Kock, *Comicorum Atticorum Fragmenta* I, pp. 112f.).

[6] *Perikeiromene* 79 (Koerte I, p. 49) = 149 (Allinson, LCL, p.214). This hanging of slaves as a punishment is to be distinguished from binding them to the block, see Aristophanes, *Equites* 1048; Eupolis, *Demoi*, see C. Austin, *Comicorum Graecorum fragmenta in papyris reperta*, p.86 (fr. 1.32); Marikas, see p. 100 (fr. 1.153).

[7] *Epistles* 2.13.3 (Schepers, pp. 39f.).

[8] Athenaeus 10, p.459a.

[9] 4.8.4; 4.9.1 (Hercher, *Erotici Scriptores Graeci* I, p. 309).

[10] *SB* 6739 = *PCZ* 59202 (Edgar II, pp.61f.), lines 7ff., letter of the *dioikētēs* Apollonius to Zeno, 254 BC: ὁ 'Αμμενεὺς εἰρηκὼς ἃ ἔγραψας πρὸς ἡμᾶς περιαχθεὶς κρεμήσεται ('If Ammeneus said what you have written, he should be brought to us and hung'). κρεμαννύναι appears several times in the sense of 'crucify', e.g. in Appian; cf. also Josephus, *BJ* 7.202; Achilles Tatius 2.37.3.

[11] U. Wilcken, *Urkunden der Ptolemäerzeit* I, Berlin 1927, no.119, line 37. Wilcken translated the word 'crucify', see the commentary, 562, in connection with Κεραμόπουλλος; there is a reference to PCZ 59202 (see n. 10 above). However, it can simply mean 'kill' here: 'a heightening of the previous ἀποκτενεῖν or only an illustration'. The same is true of O. Guéraud, *ENTEYΞΙΣ*, 1931, no.86, lines 6,8: here it is most likely to mean 'beat to death'. The difficulties of the term are reflected in Liddell and

the epitomator Justin, Pausanias, the murderer of Philip of Macedon, was arrested soon after the act and crucified; Olympias, who
instigated the murder, went by night and adorned his head with a
golden garland while he was hanging on the cross (*Epitome* 9.7.10).
The anonymous history of Alexander, *POxy* 1798 (fr.1), reports
that he was handed over to the Macedonian army for *apotympanismos*: τοῖς Μ[ακεδόσι π]αρέδωκε[ν (?). οὗτοι δ']ἀπετυπάν-
[ισαν αὐτό]ν. It is clear from this that Roman historians understood
ἀποτυ(μ)πανίζειν in terms of crucifixion.[12] In the imperial edict
against the imprisoned Christians in Lyons, AD 177 (Eusebius,
Historia Ecclesiastica 5.1.47), ἀποτυμπανίζειν has only the meaning 'to bring to death': the Roman governor then had the Roman
citizens decapitated, 'the others he sent to the beasts' (τοὺς δὲ
λοιποὺς ἔπεμπεν εἰς θηρία).

We need not dwell further on the disputed question of the
correct interpretation of *apotympanismos*, which is used in a number
of different senses, as there are sufficiently clear instances elsewhere of crucifixion being practised by and on Greeks. It has already been said that Plato and probably also Demosthenes were
familiar with this form of execution (see above, pp. 27f.). It is less

---

Scott's *A Greek-English Lexicon*. The ninth edition, ed. H. Stuart Jones
and R. McKenzie, Oxford 1940, 225, has 'crucify on a plank', which is
surely too one-sided. The supplement, ed. E. A. Barber, Oxford 1968, 21,
corrects this to 'cudgel to death'. Further meanings are 'behead' and 'kill
unmercifully, destroy'. The word can be interpreted in very different
ways, as those bound to the *tympanon* were killed in different ways. III
Maccabees 3.27 is interesting, from Ptolemy's decree against the Jews:
anyone who conceals a Jew αἰσχίσταις βασάνοις (with the most horrible
tortures) ἀποτυμπανισθήσεται πανοικίᾳ (with all his house). This could be the
threat of a form of execution similar to crucifixion. For the many different
uses of (ἀπο)τυμπανίζειν cf. J. Vergote (see bibliography), 153f. and *RAC*
VIII, 119f. At a later date it is mentioned alongside crucifixion and is
distinguished from it. Cf. also Gernet, op. cit., 291ff., 302ff.; P. Ducrey,
op. cit., 210ff.

[12] See U. Wilcken, *Alexander der Grosse und die indischen Gymno-
sophisten*, SAB, phil.-hist.-Klasse 1923 (150–83), 151ff. Wilcken reassesses
Justin's account of the crucifixion of the murderer over against the note in
Diodorus Siculus 16.94.4, who has him killed when trying to escape. He
takes up the interpretation given by Κεραμόπουλλος, 'Thus it is clear that
'ΑΠΕΤΥΠΑΝΙΣΑΝ means the punishment which Justin IX 7,10 describes
as *in cruce pendentis Pausaniae*' (152).

well known that the Athenian admiral Conon, in the service of the
satrap Pharnabazus in 397 BC, crucified the Greek leader of the
mutineers from Cyprus. In the same period, Dionysius I of Syra-
cuse crucified the Greek mercenaries of the Carthaginians whom he
took prisoner. Philip II of Macedon had hung on a gibbet the corpse
of Onomarchus, the despoiler of Delphi, who had fallen in battle.[13]
Alexander the Great carried out crucifixions on many occasions.
The fate of the able-bodied survivors of the siege of Tyre may be a
sufficient example here:[14]

> Then the wrath of the king presented a sad spectacle to the victors,
> for two thousand, for whose killing the general madness had spent
> itself, hung fixed to crosses over a huge stretch of the shore.
>
> (*Triste deinde spectaculum victoribus ira praebuit regis: II milia, in
> quibus occidendis defecerat rabies, crucibus affixi per ingens litoris
> spatium pependerunt*, Curtius Rufus, *Historia Alexandri* 4.4.17).

In the romance of Alexander it is of course the Tyrians who have
Alexander's ambassadors crucified (*Vita Alexandri* 1.35.6). Arrian's
report that Alexander hanged the rebellious Indian prince Musi-
canus 'in his own territory along with those of the Brahmans who
were the instigators of the rebellion' (*Anabasis Alexandri* 6.17.2) is
also very probably a reference to crucifixion.

The Diadochi took further the cruel practice. Perdiccas, the
administrator of the kingdom after Alexander's death, had the
Cappadocian king Ariarathes and all his relatives tortured and
crucified in 322 BC (τοῦτον . . . καὶ τοὺς συγγενεῖς αὐτοῦ
πάντας αἰκισάμενος ἀνεσταύρωσε, Diodorus Siculus 18.16.3);

---

[13] Conon: *POxy* 842 = FGH 66. XV.5. Dionysius I: Diodorus
Siculus 14.53.4. Onomarchus: Diodorus Siculus 16.61.2: κατακοπεὶς
ἐσταυρώθη; 16.35: ἐκρέμασε. This is not the case in Pausanias 10.2.5 and
Philo, *De providentia* 2.33 = Eusebius, *Praeparatio Evangelica* 8.14.33.

[14] See Justin, *Epitome* 18.3.18; Diodorus Siculus 17.16.4. See M. Hengel,
Juden, Griechen und Barbaren, SBS 76, 1976, 13. Further crucifixions
attributed to Alexander are: Curtius Rufus, *Historia Alexandri* 6.3.14; cf.
7.5.40; 7.11.28; 9.8.16 = Arrian, *Anabasis* 6.17.2; Plutarch, *Alexander*
72.3 = Arrian, *Anabasis* 7.14.4. From the Alexander romance see also the
crucifixion of the murderers of Darius by Alexander, 2.23.4 (van Thiel,
p. 104) and the threat to the ambassadors from Darius, 1.37.3 (p. 54); the
portrait of Alexander here is clearly idealized, and his cruelty is toned
down. Cf. Ducrey, op. cit., 213 and index, 242 s.v.

according to another account, however, he is said to have fallen in battle (ibid. 31.19.4). During the wars of the Diadochi mass crucifixions also came to Greece. In 314 BC the daughter-in-law of Polyperchon, the last 'administrator of Alexander's kingdom, a warlike woman', who had been given the eloquent nickname 'conqueress of cities' (κρατησίπολις), put down a rebellion in the city of Sicyon, near Corinth, and had about thirty of its inhabitants crucified (Diodorus Siculus 19.67.2). Eleven years later Demetrius Poliorcetes stormed Orchomenus in Arcadia and had its commander Strombichus killed in the same cruel way, along with about eighty of the defenders who were 'inimically disposed' towards him; however, he enlisted two thousand of the other mercenaries in his army (Diodorus Siculus 20.103.6). It may be concluded from the use of crucifixion among the Macedonians and at the time of Alexander and the Diadochi that it was also to be found in the Hellenistic monarchies, even if reports of it are sparse. We know that Antiochus III had the corpse of the usurper Molon, who had killed himself in battle, 'impaled in the most prominent place in Media' (ἀνασταυρῶσαι, Polybius 5.54.7); a similar fate was suffered by the uncle and brother-in-law of the king, Achaeus, who had set up a monarchy of his own in Asia Minor. After being betrayed into the hands of Antiochus, he was tortured to death by mutilation and his body was sewn into an ass's skin and hung (Polybius 18.21.3). At the command of Ptolemy IV, Cleomenes king of the Spartans, who had fled to Egypt and committed suicide after the failure of an attempted coup against the Ptolemies, was dishonoured in the same way (Plutarch, *Cleomenes* 38f.). There is some doubt over Justin's report that during the popular rebellion after the death of the incompetent Ptolemy IV some female members of the current court favourites were crucified (*Epitome* 30.2.7); Polybius 15.33.7ff. knows nothing of this.[15] More trust may be placed in the report in Josephus that there were also crucifixions in Judaea during the persecution of those faithful to the law at the time of the reform under Antiochus IV in 167 BC.

[15] K. Latte (see bibliography), 1606, speaks wrongly of a 'Syrian revolution'. For the death of Achaeus, Polybius 5.54.7, cf. B. A. van Proosdij, *Hermes* 69, 1934, 347–50; P. Ducrey, op. cit., 213.

His account could be based on a Hellenistic source (*Antiquitates* 12.256).[16] According to a favourite ancient anecdote, Lysimachus, one of the royal Diadochi, threatened Theodorus Atheus with crucifixion. According to Cicero's account, the latter replied:

> Make, I beg you, your abominable taunts to those purple-robed courtiers of yours; it makes no difference to Theodotus whether he rots on the ground or in the air.

> (*Istis, quaeso, ista horribilia minitare purpuratis tuis. Theodori quidem nihil interest, humine an sublime putescat, Tusculans* 1.102).[17]

A story reported by Strabo points in a similar direction. The grammarian Daphitas is said to have been crucified in Magnesia because of a derogatory epigram against the Attalid(?) kings; however, a parallel tradition in Cicero and elsewhere suggests that he was thrown down from a rock.[18]

[16] On this see E. Stauffer, *Jerusalem und Rom*, Munich 1957, 123ff. He gives an account of crucifixion in Palestine from the Persian period on (which of course needs a critical examination); also the well-considered remarks by C. D. Peddinghaus (see bibliography), 38f. Cf. also *Assumption of Moses* 8.1: *qui confitentes circumcisionem in cruce suspendit* (he crucified those who professed circumcision).

[17] The different versions of the anecdote are given in E. Mannebach, *Aristippi et Cyrenaicorum Fragmenta*, Leiden-Cologne 1961, 59f. The manner of death is not always the same. Plutarch, *Moralia* 499D, quotes the abbreviated anecdote immediately after the mention of crucifixion and impalement (see above, p. 69 n. 1); in *Moralia* 606B Theodorus is threatened with death in an iron cage. Cicero, the earliest witness, could have formulated the threat in terms of crucifixion *ad hoc*. Alexander threatens the martyr philosopher Anaxarchus the same way in *Gnomologium Vaticanum* 64. The background of the anecdote is the Cynic contempt for any form of piety towards the dead or towards funeral rites, which were so important in antiquity: see already Teles (Hense, p. 31), and the evidence given here. Seneca the Elder, *Controversiae* exc. 8.4, is typical: *Omnibus natura sepulturam dedit; naufragos fluctus, qui expulit, sepelit; suffixorum corpora a crucibus in sepulturam defluunt; eos qui vivi uruntur, poena funerat.* (Nature has given forms of burial for all: the wave which flings shipwrecked mariners into the sea also buries them; the bodies of those fastened to crosses decompose; the penalty itself incinerates those who are burnt alive.) Cf. M. Hengel, *Nachfolge und Charisma*, BZNW 34, 1968, 6 n. 16.

[18] Strabo, *Geography* 14.1.39. There is a parallel Latin tradition in Cicero, *De fato* 5; Valerius Maximus 1.8, ext. 8, cf. also *Suidae Lexicon* s.v. 'Daphitas'. The division in the tradition could derive from a confusion between κρημνέναι, 'hang', 'crucify' (Appian, *Mithridatic Wars*, 97), and κρημνίζειν, 'cast down'. For the whole question see Crusius, *PW* IV, 2134f.

Further evidence that insubordinate intellectuals had to reckon with the possibility of crucifixion under the Diadochi kings is probably to be found in an epigram which Philip V of Macedon composed as a reply to an impudent epigram composed by Alcaeus of Messene over Philip's defeat at Cynoscephalae:

> Leafless and without bark, O traveller, on this hill-top
> Stands for Alcaeus a cross, towering aloft in the sun.

> Ἄφλοιος καὶ ἄφυλλος, ὁδοιπόρε, τῷδ' ἐπὶ νώτῳ
>   Ἀλκαίῳ σταυρὸς πήγνυται ἠλίβατος

(Plutarch, *Titus Flaminius* 9.4).

Here the king threatens the poet with a gruesome fate should he fall into his hands. These examples show that even in the pre-Roman, Hellenistic period, crucifixion was not unknown as a punishment for state criminals in the Greek-speaking East as well. On the other hand, clear instances of the crucifixion of slaves only occur more frequently under Roman rule.

The epitaph of a master murdered by his slave, from Amysos in Caria, finally records that the citizens of the town – and not the Roman authorities – 'hung the murderer alive for the wild beasts and birds of prey'.[19] It dates from the second or first century BC. Roman influence may already be evident here, since in 133 BC Attalus III had made over his kingdom to the Romans.

Whereas it seems clear so far that crucifixion and impalement – the two are closely connected – appear in connection with crimes of *lèse-majesté* and high treason, or in the context of acts of war, in the Roman period this form of execution appears more frequently as a punishment for slaves and violent criminals from among the population of the provinces. H.-W. Kuhn's conclusion, drawn from the relatively few reports of crucifixion in Greece and Asia

---

[19] *The Collection of Ancient Greek Inscriptions in the British Museum* IV, 2, ed. F. H. Marshall, 1916, no. 1036: ἀλλὰ πολῖται ἐμοὶ τὸν ἐμὲ ῥέξαντα τοιαῦτα θηροὶ καὶ οἰωνοῖς ζωὸν ἀνεκρέμασαν. Cf. K. Latte (see bibliography), 1606; for the 'hanging' of slaves see above, p. 71. The text of the inscription also appears in L. Robert, *Études Anatoliennes* 3, Paris 1937, 389 n. o. M. Rostovtzeff, *The Social and Economic History of the Hellenistic World* III, London 1941, 1521 n.76, asks whether this execution may not have taken place in connection with the slave revolt of Aristonicus. However, what we have here is an individual action: the slave had killed his master Demetrius, who had got drunk at a banquet, and set fire to the house.

Minor during the first 150 years of the common era, is misleading; it is not the case 'that crucifixion was not perhaps as frequent as is usually supposed in this important missionary area of early Christianity'.[20] First, we have relatively few sources from this period. For orators like Dio Chrysostom,[21] Aristides or Maximus of Tyre, or learned writers like Plutarch, the crucifixion of slaves and robbers was an unappetizing theme; still, Plutarch knew well enough that 'every criminal condemned to death bears his cross on his back' (καὶ τῷ μὲν σώματι τῶν κολαζομένων ἕκαστος κακούργων ἐκφέρει τὸν αὑτοῦ σταυρόν).[22] Honorific inscriptions and epitaphs also had other things to record than cruel executions. However, the 'completely certain evidence'[23] that we lack is abundantly supplied by the Greek romances, the satires of Lucian the Syrian, the treatise on dreams by Artemidorus of Ephesus,[24] the medical[25] and not least the astrological literature, where the constellation of Andromeda brought an especial threat of the cross. Bad nativities in connection with Mars and Saturn also threatened crucifixion and other *summa supplicia*.[26] Here there were fewer

[20] H.-W. Kuhn (see bibliography), 10.

[21] He mentions only the classic case of Polycrates (17.15, see above p. 24): 'he met with no easy death, but was crucified by that barbarian and thus perished' (μηδὲ ῥᾳδίου γε θανάτου τυχεῖν, ἀλλ' ἀνασκολοπισθέντα ὑπὸ τοῦ βαρβάρου διαφθαρῆναι).

[22] Plutarch, *Moralia* 554A/B; cf. 554D: στρεβλοῦν ἢ κρεμαννύναι τὸν πονηρόν. See also p. 69 n. 1 above on 499D.

[23] H.-W. Kuhn, op. cit. The term 'completely certain evidence' as applied to ancient history needs to be defined here. There are only various degrees of probability.

[24] Artemidorus, *Oneirocriticon* 1.76; 2.53; 2.68; 4.33; 4.49. Even in the late dream book by Achmes, *Oneirocriticon* 90 (Drexel, pp. 54f.), the theme of crucifixion as a form of execution appears in various modes.

[25] Galen, *De Usu Partium* 12.11 (Helmreich II, p.214): ἢ σταυρῷ προσηλωμένον; cf. also the unburied bodies of robbers put on display on a hillside, on which Galen was able to pursue anatomical studies: *De Anatomicis Administrationibus* 3 (Kühn II, p. 385).

[26] Andromeda: Manilius, *Astronomica* 5.553: *et cruce uirginea moritura puella pependit* (and the virgin maiden hung dying on the cross). Cf. *Liber Hermetis Trismegisti* XXV, ed. Gundel, AAM phil.-hist. Abteilung, NF 12, 1936, p. 51, 25f.: *crucifixos facit propter Andromedam; Catalogus Codicum Astrologorum Graecorum* VIII.1, ed. F. Cumont, 1929, p. 248.16ff. Mars and Saturn: *Liber Hermetis . . .* XXVI, p. 79, 26–32: *Saturnus et Mars in ascendente . . .; et natus malum coniugium habebit et ipse erit pravus mali*

aesthetic constraints about calling a spade a spade: the atmosphere
here was closest to the reality of everyday life and thus to the
thoughts and feelings of ordinary people. One might go on to ask

---

*consilii . . . et plures eorum moriuntur a daemonibus . . . quoniam et cruc(i)
plures affixi mortui sunt et decollati sunt vel mutilati sunt membra vel vivi
combusti fuerunt* (the one born when Saturn and Mars are in the ascendant
will have a bad marriage and he himself will be wicked and of evil counsel
. . . and many of them will die from demons . . . since many have died
fastened to crosses or have been decapitated or their limbs have been
mutilated or they have been burnt alive); they are very dangerous for the
fugitive slave: *Catalogus Codicum Graecorum* V.3, ed. I. Heeg, 1910, p.84.
29f.: ἐὰν δὲ ὁ μὲν Ἄρης ἐκ τῶν εὐωνύμων, ὁ δὲ Κρόνος ἐκ τῶν δεξιῶν αὐτὴν περιέχωσιν,
ὁ φυγὼν ἀνασταυρωθήσεται (If [the moon] is between Ares on the left and
Cronos on the right, the fugitive will be crucified). Firmicus Maternus,
Mathesis 6.31.58 (Kroll/Skutsch II, 164): '*Si vero cum his Saturnus fuerit
inventus, ipse nobis exitium mortis ostendit. Nam (in) istis facinoribus
deprehensus severa animadvertentis sententia patibulo subfixus in crucem
tollitur*' (But if Saturn is found in conjunction with these, it shows us a
deadly fate. For those who are detected in such crimes are punished with a
severe sentence, fastened to the stake and crucified). See also *Catalogus*
VIII.1, ed. F. Cumont, 1929, p.176, 15f., for the case of a very bad
constellation: καὶ ἀνασταυρούμενον δηλοῦσι, τὸν τοιοῦτον (i.e. λῃστήν . . . καὶ
ἀνδροφόνον) (and they show that such a man [i.e. a robber . . . and murderer]
will be crucified); op.cit. VIII.4, ed. P. Boudreaux-F. Cumont, 1922, p.
200, 12f.: μαρτυρηθεὶς δὲ ὁ Ἄρης ὑπὸ Ἡλίου, ἀπὸ δήμου ἤ πλήθους ἤ βασιλέων ἀναιρεῖ
σταυρουμένους ἤ ἀποκεφαλιζομένους ἤ θηριομαχοῦντας (shown by Ares under the
sun that they will be crucified or beheaded or put to the beasts by the
people or by the rabble or by kings); p.201.22f.: ὁ Κρόνος ὑπογείῳ, Ἄρης
μεσουρανῶν νυκτὸς ποιοῦσιν ἐσταυρωμένους καὶ ὑπὸ ὄρνεων βεβρωμένους (Cronos at
its nadir and Ares in mid-heaven by night indicate those who are crucified
and eaten by birds); cf. op. cit. IX.1, ed. S. Weinstock, 1951, p.150.23f.:
μετὰ σπονδύλου ἀνθρώπου ἐσταυρωμένου (with the vertebra of a crucified man).
Firmicus Maternus, *Mathesis* 6.31.73 (II.169); 8.6.11 (II.298: *aut tolluntur
in crucem, aut crura illis publica animadversione franguntur* (they are either
crucified or their legs are broken by public sentence); 8.22.3 (II, 237), see
above p. 49; 8.25.6 (II, 333f.): *In XVIII parte Librae quicumque habuerit
horoscopum, in crucem iussu imperatoris tolletur, aut praesente imperatore
torquebitur, aut iussu principali suspendetur* (anyone who has the ascendant
in the eighteenth degree of Libra will be crucified at the order of the
emperor or will be tortured in the presence of the emperor or will be hung
on his orders). But there was not only the possibility that the emperor
might have citizens crucified. Under the constellation of Mars and the
moon a tyrant could meet with the same fate: *Catalogus* XI.1, ed. C. O.
Zuretti, 1932, p.259.8: τὸν τύραννον ἑαυτὸν ἀπαρτᾶν λέγε ἤ σταυρούμενον. Cf. also
F. Cumont, op. cit. (above p. 9 n. 20), 296ff., and Pseudo-Manetho,
Apotelesmatica 1.148f.; 4.197ff.; 5.219ff., see n. 20 above.

what 'completely certain evidence' – which Kuhn misses for the
East – we have for crucifixion in this period from Roman Gaul,
from Spain – apart from the one account about Galba (see above,
p.40), North Africa and the Danube provinces. There, too, was it
only a very rare form of execution? Lastly, the very places which
were the centres of Paul's activity were also centres of Roman
power. Corinth, Philippi, Troas, Pisidian Antioch, Lystra and
Iconium (this last at least from the time of Hadrian) were Roman
colonies, and in Syrian Antioch, Ephesus, Thessalonica and
Corinth there were Roman provincial governors who followed
Roman legal practice, especially in capital cases. As a Roman
citizen, Paul himself will have been well informed about the execution of Roman justice and his own rights as a citizen (Acts 25.11f.).
Moreover, from the evidence that we have for crucifixion in the
Greek-speaking provinces, we may conclude that the cross was
very well known to every slave and peasant in this part of the
empire also. Attitudes to it may have been different. The Palestinian
peasant, his sympathies with the freedom movement, saw in it the
feared and hated instrument of repression employed by his Roman
overlords, whereas the majority of the inhabitants of the Greek
cities will have regarded it as a horrible but nevertheless necessary
instrument for the preservation of law and order against robbers,
violent men and rebellious slaves. In the East, in particular, the
end of the Civil War and the beginning of the Principate brought
great relief, increased security and economic revival, which was
highly esteemed by the urban population.

Moreover, on the whole the evidence for crucifixion in this area
is not as sparse as all that. In 97 BC, Q. Mucius Scaevola, as proconsul of Asia, had a slave and chief agent of the tax farmers
executed on the cross immediately before he was due to be freed
(Diodorus Siculus 37.5.3).[27] During the First Mithridatic War, in
88 BC, after the capture of the island of Sciathos, Q. Bruttius Sura
had crucified slaves who were in the service of Mithridates (Appian,
Mithridatic Wars 29). The execution of pirates by the young Caesar

[27] Freeing him would have made the *servile supplicium* impossible, see
above pp. 44f. For the crucifixions of Mithridates VI of Pontus, see above,
p. 23 n. 11.

in Pergamon about 75 BC is well known.[28] Suetonius (*Iulius* 74.1)
has the interesting but probably secondary version that with his
proverbial clemency Caesar had the pirates' throats cut before
crucifixion in order to spare them suffering (*iugulari prius iussit,
deinde suffigi*). In AD 44 Claudius restricted the freedom of the island
state of Rhodes because the Rhodians 'had crucified some Romans'
(ὅτι Ῥωμαίους τινὰς ἀνεσκολόπισαν, Dio Cassius 60.24.4). As a
civitas foederata atque libera, which had been a faithful ally of Rome
for almost 250 years, Rhodes had independent capital justice. The
background to this event is, however, obscure.[29] According to
Suetonius, Domitian had Hermogenes, a writer from Tarsus,
executed because of some objectionable allusions in one of his
books, while the unfortunate slaves who had written it out were
crucified out of hand (*Domitian* 10.1).[30] As evidence from Egypt
I have found the report of a trial from the first century AD; unfortunately the text is very fragmentary. It contains a hearing of
four defendants before a high Roman official, presumably in Alexandria. One of the accused is to be flogged, and there is a mention
of crucifixion towards the end (σταυροποίαν [π]είσεται).[31] The

[28] Plutarch, *Caesar* 2.2–4; Valerius Maximus 6.9.15.

[29] Dio Cassius 60.24.2. M. P. Charlesworth, *CAH* X, ²1952, 682,
conjectures 'a riot in which some Roman citizens were crucified'; similarly
D. Magie, *Roman Rule in Asia Minor* I, Princeton 1950, 548. In II, 1406,
Magie conjectures an identification with the *seditio* which Tacitus, *Annals*
12.58.2, reports for AD 53: *redditur Rhodiis libertas, adempta saepe aut
firmata, prout bellis externis meruerant aut domi seditione deliquerant* (The
Rhodians recovered their liberties, so often forfeited or confirmed as the
balance varied between their military service abroad and their serious
offences at home). Possibly this *seditio* merely consisted in the fact that the
people of Rhodes wanted to show their power of jurisdiction as a *civitas
libera*.

[30] It remains obscure whether this happened in Rome or somewhere
in the East.

[31] *POxy* 2339; this is evidently a genuine account of the proceedings.
That no crucifixion appears in the literary *Acta Alexandrinorum* can be
explained, in my view, by the fact that this despised form of execution
was below the status of the respected citizens of Alexandria who are
celebrated here. From the time of the Ptolemies onwards there were two
forms of flogging as a punishment practised in Alexandria. The worse
kind, scourging, was only carried out on criminals from the lower classes.
Flaccus punished the thirty-eight members of the Jewish Gerousia in this

editor connects the text with unrest among the Greeks and
Jews during which, according to Josephus, there were numerous
executions. This, of course, only made matters worse (*BJ* 2.489).
For the time of Caligula Philo reports torture and crucifixions of
Jews in the amphitheatre of the Egyptian capital (*In Flaccum* 72,
84f.). In the romance of Xenophon of Ephesus, which probably
comes from the second century AD, the prefect of Egypt has the
unfortunate hero crucified on a false charge; however, in a miraculous way the crucified man is rescued by the divine Nile, and the
woman who has denounced him (and has murdered her husband)
suffers the due penalty.[32]

A brief word should also be said about the Greek romances
generally. Crucifixion of the hero or heroine is part of their stock in
trade, and only a higher form of this 'recreational literature', as
represented say by Heliodorus' *Aethiopica*, scorns such cruelty. In
the *Babyloniaca* written by the Syrian Iamblichus, the hero is
twice overtaken by this fearful punishment, but on both occasions
he is taken down from the cross and freed.[33] Habrocomes, the chief
figure in the romance by Xenophon of Ephesus which has already
been mentioned, is first tortured almost to death and later crucified.
Even his beloved, Anthea, is in danger of being crucified after she
has killed a robber in self-defence.[34] However, heroes cannot on
any account be allowed to suffer such a painful and shameful
death – this can only befall evil-doers.[35] Chariton of Aphrodisias,

---

way (Philo, *In Flaccum* 75). In the account of the trial one of the accused
with an Egyptian name protests against the flogging: he claims that it is
against the law and threatens success in war. The alleged crucifixion mentioned by R. Taubenschlag, *The Law of Greco-Roman Egypt in the Light
of the Papyri*, Warsaw ²1955, 434 n.25 (BGU 1024.8–11) is in fact an
execution by the sword. Of course we have only a very few accounts of
capital cases from Egypt.

[32] *Ephesiaca* 4.2.1ff.; 4.4.2 (Hercher, *Erotici Scriptores Graeci* I,
pp. 374f.).

[33] Iamblichus, *Babyloniaca* 2 and 21 (Hercher I, pp. 221, 229), according to Photius, *Bibliotheca*.

[34] Xenophon, *Ephesiaca* 2.6; 4.2.1ff.; 4.6.2 (Hercher I, pp. 351f., 374f.,
378).

[35] Ibid., 4.4.2 (Hercher I, p. 277): Cyno, who murdered her husband;
Chariton 3.4.18 (Hercher II, p. 57): the robber Theron at the tomb of

who was perhaps still writing in the first century AD, gives a vivid description of crucifixion as a punishment for slaves: sixteen slaves from the domains of the satrap Mithridates escaped from their lodgings, but were recaptured and, chained together by necks and feet, were led to the place of execution, each carrying his own cross. 'The executioners supplemented the necessary death penalty by other wretched practices such as were effective as an example to the rest(of the slaves)', i.e. the whole proceedings were designed above all as a deterrent. The hero of the romance is saved at the last moment, just before he is to be nailed to the cross.[36]

There are further indications of the relatively frequent use of crucifixion. Lucian, for example in his portrayal of the arrival of the dead in the underworld,[37] or a pseudonymous letter of Diogenes,[38]

Callirhoe, whom he has sold to slave-dealers; cf. the crucifixion of the murderers of Darius on the tomb of the dead ruler in the Alexander romance, see above, p. 73 n. 14.

[36] Chariton 4.2.6ff.; 4.3.3ff.; cf. 5.10.6 (II, pp.72f., 75, 103). K. Kerényi, *Die griechisch-orientalische Romanliteratur in religionsgeschicht-licher Beleuchtung*, Darmstadt ²1962, investigates the theme of crucifixion and suffering in the Greek romances in detail (109ff.; 123ff.; delivery from the cross and transfiguration). However, his idea that the ancient Egyptian Ded-column of Osiris underlies the theme of the cross (110ff.) and his introduction of gnostic writings are misleading. The ancient romance writers wanted to introduce tension into their stories with 'crime, sex and religion', but they were not concealing any mysteries. The verdict of R. Merkelbach, *Roman und Mysterium in der Antike*, Munich and Berlin 1962, 180, is more restrained: he seeks to see crucifixion as an 'initiation test' (cf. 191). However, this too is improbable. Crucifixion simply represents the supreme threat to the hero, and screws up tension to the highest pitch. See the criticism of Kerényi in A. D. Nock, *Essays on Religion and the Ancient World* I, ed. Z. Stewart, Oxford 1972, 170, who rightly points out that crucifixion plays no part in the mysteries: Osiris was not crucified.

[37] *Cataplous* 6: τοὺς ἐκ δικαστηρίου . . . παράγαγε, λέγω δὲ τοὺς ἐκ τυμπάνου καὶ τοὺς ἀνεσκολοπισμένους (Bring in the output of the courts, I mean those who died by the *tympanon* and by the cross), cf. also *De morte Peregrini* 45 and Sextus Empiricus, *Adversus Mathematicos* 2.30, where crucifixion is missing and there is mention only of prison and the *tympanon*.

[38] Diogenes, *Epistle* 28.3 (Hercher, p.242): οὔκουν πολλοὶ μὲν ἐπὶ τῶν σταυρῶν κρέμανται, πολλοὶ δὲ ὑπὸ τοῦ δημίου ἀπεσφαγμένοι (many are hung on the cross and many have their throats cut by the executioner). Cf. the anecdote ascribed to him, Diogenes Laertius, *Vita Philosophorum* 6.45.

indicate that its significance in the Greek-speaking world was by no means inconsiderable. In Lucian's dialogue *Piscator* (ch.2), the philosophers are summoned by Socrates to consider how they are to kill the free-thinking Parrhesiades. The first proposal from the assembled company is, 'I think he should be crucified'; the next speaker agrees: 'Yes, by Zeus, but before that he must be flogged'; there then follows putting out his eyes and cutting off his tongue. There could be a distant allusion here to Plato's just man crucified (see above, p.28). At all events, death by crucifixion seems to be taken for granted as the *summum supplicium*. On the basis of the examples given here, which could certainly be multiplied further, we may conclude that in the Greek-speaking East crucifixion was no less well-known, feared and abhorred than in the Latin West – particularly among the lower classes.[39]

All this leads to a final conclusion which it is difficult to resist. When Paul spoke in his mission preaching about the 'crucified Christ' (I Corinthians 1.23; 2.2; Galatians 3.1), every hearer in the Greek-speaking East between Jerusalem and Illyria (Romans 15.19) knew that this 'Christ' – for Paul the title was already a proper name – had suffered a particularly cruel and shameful death, which as a rule was reserved for hardened criminals, rebellious slaves and rebels against the Roman state. That this crucified Jew, Jesus Christ, could truly be a divine being sent on earth, God's Son, the Lord of all and the coming judge of the world, must inevitably have been thought by any educated man to be utter 'madness' and presumptuousness.

[39] I have deliberately left aside instances where crucifixion seems to have been introduced secondarily into the earlier Greek traditions, e.g. in the two fables of Hyginus, no.194 on the zither player Arion and the pirates, and no.257 on Phalaris of Selinunte and the two Pythagorean friends, which Schiller turned into his famous ballad 'Die Bürgschaft'.

Crucifixion among the Jews

The history of crucifixion in Judaea and in the Jewish tradition really needs a separate investigation; I have therefore deliberately kept the μωρία of the cross among the 'Gentiles' (I Corinthians 1.23) in the foreground. H.-W. Kuhn is quite right in stressing that the σκάνδαλον τοῦ σταυροῦ for the Jews according to I Corinthians 1.23; Galatians 5.11 has a religious character going back to Deuteronomy 21.23.[1] Y. Yadin has demonstrated by means of the Qumran temple scroll that in the Hellenistic-Hasmonean period crucifixion was practised as the form of death penalty applied in cases of high treason – probably for this very reason; it was taken over from the non-Jewish world. The *arbori infelici suspendere* in severe cases of *perduellio* in Rome is something of an analogy here.[2] Anyone who had betrayed his own people to a foreign enemy had to be subjected to the utmost dishonour. This explains the crucifixion of 800 Pharisees by Alexander Jannaeus[3] and the remarkable report, already handed down in the Mishnah, that Simeon b. Shetah had seventy or eighty 'sorceresses' 'hung' in Ashkelon; in my view what we have here is a polemical encipherment of the

---

[1] H.-W. Kuhn (see bibliography), 36f.

[2] Y. Yadin, *Pesher Nahum* (see bibliography). The objections made by J. M. Baumgarten (see bibliography) are not at all convincing.

[3] Josephus, *BJ* 1.97f.; *Antiquitates* 13.380–3, cf. *BJ* 1.113; *Antiquitates* 13.410f.; see J. M. Allegro, *Qumran Cave 4*, I, DJDJ V, 1968, 37–42, no. 169; 4QpNah 3–4 col. I.4–9; see also J. Strugnell, 'Notes en marge du volume V des "Discoveries in the Judaean Desert of Jordan"', *RdQ* 7, 1969–71, (163–276) 207. For Jannaeus' banquet before those who were crucified see Iamblichus, *Babyloniaca* 21 (Hercher I, p.229): King Garmos, garlanded and dancing, holds a banquet with flute-players in front of the hero's cross. For the killing of women and children before the eyes of those who were crucified see Herodotus 4.202.1 and 9.120.4.

Pharisaic counter-reaction against the Sanhedrin after the death of Alexander Jannaeus, under queen Salome, when the Pharisees who had reached positions of power in the state took vengeance on the Sadducean advisers of the dead king and repaid them with like for like. The proud Sadducean priests and officers were transformed into pagan witches in a radical polemical transformation. The striking thing about this anecdote is that Ashkelon was the only city in Palestine which the Hasmoneans had not sacked.[4]

It is all the more significant that Herod broke with this tradition of execution and it can hardly be a coincidence that not a single crucifixion is reported by Josephus from his time. Did the king want to dissociate himself from Hasmonean custom? This mass murderer would surely not have had humane considerations in mind. The excessive use made of crucifixion by the Romans in the pacification of Judaea meant that from the beginning of direct Roman rule crucifixion was taboo as a form of the Jewish death penalty. This change can also be inferred from rabbinic interpretation of Deuteronomy 21.23. Varus had already had two thousand prisoners crucified around Jerusalem,[5] and AD 70, the year of terror, brought a sorry climax in this respect too. Nevertheless, the cross never became the symbol of Jewish suffering; the influence of Deuteronomy 21.23 made this impossible. So a crucified messiah could not be accepted either. It was here that the preaching of the earliest Christians caused particular offence in the mother country itself. It also explains why the theme of the crucified faithful plays no part in Jewish legends about martyrs. The cross had become too much a sign of the passion of Jesus and his followers – though in the Talmudic literature we have a whole series of references to the crucifixion of Jews during the later empire.

[4] Mishnah, *Sanhedrin* 6.5, cf. *j.Sanh.* 23c. This tradition, which completely contradicts the whole of the later rabbinic legal tradition, cannot be pure invention. I regard it as a tradition which has been encoded in the interests of polemic. Those in the know would be fully aware of its meaning. Josephus, *BJ* 1.113, and above all *Antiquitates* 13.410f., shows that the Pharisees took bloody revenge. For 'hanging' as a punishment for high treason see also Targum Jonathan II on Num. 25.4; M. Hengel, *Nachfolge und Charisma*, BZNW 34, 1968, 64 n.77.

[5] See p. 26 n. 17 above. Cf. *Assumption of Moses* 6.9: *aliquos crucifigit circa coloniam eorum.*

12

Summary

I have attempted to give a survey of the use of crucifixion as a penalty in the Graeco-Roman world, as a contribution towards a better understanding of Paul's remark about the μωρία of the λόγος τοῦ σταυροῦ. The following points may be made in conclusion. I am well aware that this study remains essentially incomplete, for now at the end I should really begin all over again with a detailed exegesis of the evidence about the cross in the writings of Paul. As it is, I am breaking off where theological work proper ought to begin. The preceding chapters are no more than 'historical preliminaries' for a presentation of the *theologia crucis* in Paul. The reader must therefore excuse me if I now do no more than hint at some of the theological lines which mark out the further possibilities of progress, along with a summary of the historical results.

1. Crucifixion as a penalty was remarkably widespread in antiquity. It appears in various forms among numerous peoples of the ancient world, even among the Greeks. There was evidently neither the desire nor the power to abolish it, even where people were fully aware of its extreme cruelty. It thus formed a harsh contradiction to the idealistic picture of antiquity which was inaugurated by Winckelmann in terms of 'noble simplicity and quiet greatness' (*edle Einfalt und stille Grösse*). Our own age, which is proud of its humanity and its progress, but which sees the use of the death penalty, torture and terror increasing in the world rather than decreasing, can hardly pride itself on having overcome this ancient contradiction.

2. Crucifixion was and remained a political and military punishment. While among the Persians and the Carthaginians it was

imposed primarily on high officials and commanders, as on rebels, among the Romans it was inflicted above all on the lower classes, i.e. slaves, violent criminals and the unruly elements in rebellious provinces, not least in Judaea.

3. The chief reason for its use was its allegedly supreme efficacy as a deterrent; it was, of course, carried out publicly. As a rule the crucified man was regarded as a criminal who was receiving just and necessary punishment. There was doubtless a fear that to give up this form of execution might undermine the authority of the state and existing law and order.

4. At the same time, crucifixion satisfied the primitive lust for revenge and the sadistic cruelty of individual rulers and of the masses. It was usually associated with other forms of torture, including at least flogging. At relatively small expense and to great public effect the criminal could be tortured to death for days in an unspeakable way. Crucifixion is thus a specific expression of the inhumanity dormant within men which these days is expressed, for example, in the call for the death penalty, for popular justice and for harsher treatment of criminals, as an expression of retribution. It is a manifestation of trans-subjective evil, a form of execution which manifests the demonic character of human cruelty and bestiality.

5. By the public display of a naked victim at a prominent place – at a crossroads, in the theatre, on high ground, at the place of his crime – crucifixion also represented his uttermost humiliation, which had a numinous dimension to it. With Deuteronomy 21.23 in the background, the Jew in particular was very aware of this. This form of execution, more than any other, had associations with the idea of human sacrifice, which was never completely suppressed in antiquity. The sacrifice of countless hordes of people in our century to national idols or to the 'correct' political view shows that this irrational demand for human sacrifice can be found even today.

6. Crucifixion was aggravated further by the fact that quite often its victims were never buried. It was a stereotyped picture that the crucified victim served as food for wild beasts and birds of prey. In this way his humiliation was made complete. What it meant for a man in antiquity to be refused burial, and the dishonour which

went with it, can hardly be appreciated by modern man.

7. In Roman times, crucifixion was practised above all on dangerous criminals and members of the lowest classes. These were primarily people who had been outlawed from society or slaves who on the whole had no rights, in other words, groups whose development had to be suppressed by all possible means to safeguard law and order in the state. Because large strata of the population welcomed the security and the world-wide peace which the empire brought with it, the crucified victim was defamed both socially and ethically in popular awareness, and this impression was heightened still further by the religious elements involved.

8. Relatively few attempts at criticism or even at a philosophical development of the theme of the boundless suffering of countless victims of crucifixion can be found. At best, we can see it in the Stoic preaching of the ἀπάθεια and ἀρετή, the calmness and virtue of the wise man, where in some circumstances the torment of the man dying on the cross could be used as a metaphor. Here crucifixion became a simile for the suffering from which the wise man can free himself only by death, which delivers the soul from the body to which it is tied. In the romances, on the other hand, crucifixion made for exciting entertainment and sensationalism. Here the suffering was not really taken seriously. The accounts of the crucifixion of the hero served to give the reader a thrill: the tension was then resolved by the freeing of the crucified victim and the obligatory happy ending.

9. In this context, the earliest Christian message of the crucified messiah demonstrated the 'solidarity' of the love of God with the unspeakable suffering of those who were tortured and put to death by human cruelty, as this can be seen from the ancient sources. This suffering has continued down to the present century in a 'passion story' which we cannot even begin to assess, a 'passion story' which is based on human sin, in which we all without exception participate, as beings who live under the power of death. In the person and the fate of the one man Jesus of Nazareth this saving 'solidarity' of God with us is given its historical and physical form. In him, the 'Son of God', God himself took up the 'existence of a slave' and died the 'slaves' death' on the tree of martyrdom (Philippians 2.8), given up

to public shame (Hebrews 12.2) and the 'curse of the law' (Galatians 3.13), so that in the 'death of God' life might win victory over death. In other words, in the death of Jesus of Nazareth God identified himself with the extreme of human wretchedness, which Jesus endured as a representative of us all, in order to bring us to the freedom of the children of God:

> He who did not spare his own Son,
> but gave him up for us all,
> will he not also give us all things with him? (Romans 8.32)

This radical kenosis of God was the revolutionary new element in the preaching of the gospel. It caused offence, but in this very offence it revealed itself as the centre of the gospel. For the death of Jesus on the cross is very much more than a religious symbol, say of the uttermost readiness of a man for suffering and sacrifice; it is more than just an ethical model which calls for discipleship, though it is all this *as well*. What we have here is God's communication of himself, the free action through which he establishes the effective basis of our salvation. In ancient thought, e.g. among the Stoics, an ethical and symbolic interpretation of the crucifixion was still possible, but to assert that God himself accepted death in the form of a crucified Jewish manual worker from Galilee in order to break the power of death and bring salvation to all men could only seem folly and madness to men of ancient times. Even now, any genuine theology will have to be measured against the test of this scandal.

10. When Paul talks of the 'folly' of the message of the crucified Jesus, he is therefore not speaking in riddles or using an abstract cipher. He is expressing the harsh experience of his missionary preaching and the offence that it caused, in particular the experience of his preaching among non-Jews, with whom his apostolate was particularly concerned. The reason why in his letters he talks about the cross above all in a polemical context is that he deliberately wants to provoke his opponents, who are attempting to water down the offence caused by the cross. Thus in a way the 'word of the cross' is the spearhead of his message. And because Paul still understands the cross as the real, cruel instrument of execution, as the instrument of the bloody execution of Jesus, it is impossible to

dissociate talk of the atoning death of Jesus or the blood of Jesus from this 'word of the cross'. The spearhead cannot be broken off the spear. Rather, the complex of the death of Jesus is a single entity for the apostle, in which he never forgets the fact that Jesus did not die a gentle death like Socrates, with his cup of hemlock, much less passing on 'old and full of years' like the patriarchs of the Old Testament. Rather, he died like a slave or a common criminal, in torment, on the tree of shame. Paul's Jesus did not die just any death; he was 'given up for us all' on the cross, in a cruel and a contemptible way.

The theological reasoning of our time shows very clearly that the particular form of the death of Jesus, the man and the messiah, represents a scandal which people would like to blunt, remove or domesticate in any way possible. We shall have to guarantee the truth of our theological thinking at this point. Reflection on the harsh reality of crucifixion in antiquity may help us to overcome the acute loss of reality which is to be found so often in present theology and preaching.

BIBLIOGRAPHY

I. Barkan, *Capital Punishment in Ancient Athens*, Chicago 1936

J. M. Baumgarten, 'Does *tlh* in the Temple Scroll refer to Crucifixion?', *JBL* 91, 1972, 472–81

E. Benz, *Der gekreuzigte Gerechte bei Plato, im Neuen Testament und in der alten Kirche*, AAMz 1950, no. 12

J. Blinzler, *Der Prozess Jesu*, Regensburg ⁴1969; ET of 2nd ed., *The Trial of Jesus*, Westminster, Md, 1959

E. Brandenburger, 'Σταυρός, Kreuzigung Jesu und Kreuzestheologie', *WuD* NF 10, 1969, 17–43

E. Dinkler, 'Jesu Wort vom Kreuztragen', *Signum Crucis. Aufsätze zum Neuen Testament und zur Christlichen Archäologie*, Tübingen 1967, 77–98

id., 'Das Kreuz als Siegeszeichen', ibid., 55–76

id., 'Kreuzzeichen und Kreuz. Tav, Chi und Stauros', ibid., 26–54

id., 'Zur Geschichte des Kreuzsymbols', ibid., 1–25

P. Ducrey, *Le traitement des prisonniers de guerre dans la Grèce antique, des origines à la conquête romaine*, Paris 1968

id., 'Note sur la crucifixion', *MusHelv* 28, 1971, 183–5

H. Fulda, *Das Kreuz und die Kreuzigung. Eine antiquarische Untersuchung . . .*, Breslau 1878

P. Garnsey, *Social Status and Legal Privilege in the Roman Empire*, Oxford 1970

L. Gernet, *Anthropologie de la Grèce antique*, Paris 1968, 288–329

E. Grässer, '"Der politisch gekreuzigte Christus". Kritische Anmerkungen zu einer politischen Hermeneutik des Evangeliums', in *Text und Situation. Gesammelte Aufsätze zum Neuen Testament*, Gütersloh 1973, 302–30

M. Hengel, *The Son of God. The Origin of Christology and the History of Jewish-Hellenistic Religion*, ET London and Philadelphia 1976

H. F. Hitzig, 'Crux', *PW* IV, 1901, 1728–31

M. Kähler, 'Das Kreuz. Grund und Mass der Christologie', *Schriften zur Christologie und Mission. Gesamtausgabe der Schriften zur Mission*, ed. H. Frohnes, ThB 42, 1971, 292–350

E. Käsemann, 'Die Gegenwart des Gekreuzigten', in *Deutscher Evangelischer Kirchentag Hannover 1967. Dokumente*, Hanover 1967, 424–37, cf. 438–62 id., 'The Saving Significance of the Death of Jesus in Paul', *Perspectives on Paul*, ET London and Philadelphia 1971, 32–59

'Α. Δ. Κεραμόπουλλος, 'Ο ἀποτυμπανισμός. Συμβολὴ ἀρχαιολογικὴ εἰς τὴν ἱστορίαν τοῦ ποινικοῦ δικαίου καὶ τὴν λαογραφίαν, Βιβλιοθήκη τῆς ἐν 'Αθήναις 'Αρχαιολογικῆς 'Εταιρείας 22, Athens 1923

G. Klein, 'Das Ärgernis des Kreuzes', in *Ärgernisse. Konfrontationen mit dem Neuen Testament*, Munich 1970, 115–31

H.-W. Kuhn, 'Jesus als Gekreuzigter in der frühchristlicher Verkündigung bis zur Mitte des 2. Jahrhunderts', *ZTK* 72, 1975, 1–46

K. Latte, 'Todesstrafe', *PW* Suppl VII, 1940, 1599–1619

H.-G. Link, 'Gegenwärtige Probleme einer Kreuzestheologie. Ein Bericht', *EvTh* 33, 1973, 337–45

A. W. Lintott, *Violence in Ancient Rome*, Oxford 1968

J. Lipsius, *De Cruce libri tres*, Amsterdam 1670

W. Marxsen, 'Erwägungen zum Problem des verkündigten Kreuzes', *NTS* 8, 1961/62, 204–14

J. Moltmann, *The Crucified God*, ET London and New York 1974

T. Mommsen, *Römisches Strafrecht*, 1899 reprinted Berlin 1955

F.-J. Ortkemper, *Das Kreuz in der Verkündigung des Apostels Paulus. Dargestellt an den Texten der paulinischen Hauptbriefe*, SBS 24, [2]1968

C. D. Peddinghaus, *Die Entstehung der Leidensgeschichte. Eine traditionsgeschichtliche und historische Untersuchung des Werdens und Wachsens der erzählenden Passionstradition bis zum Entwurf des Markus*, Diss. Heidelberg 1965 (typescript)

G. Q. Reijners, *The Terminology of the Holy Cross in Early Christian Literature as based upon Old Testament Typology*, Diss. Nijmegen 1965

L. Ruppert, *Jesus als der leidende Gerechte? Der Weg Jesu im Lichte eines alt- und zwischentestamentlichen Motivs*, SBS 59, 1972

J. Schneider, σταυρός κτλ., *TDNT* VII, 1971, 572–84

W. Schrage, 'Leid, Kreuz und Eschaton. Die Peristasenkataloge als Merkmale paulinischer *theologia crucis* und Eschatologie', *EvTh* 34, 1974, 141–75

J. Stockbauer, *Kunstgeschichte des Kreuzes. Die bildliche Darstellung des Erlösungstodes Christi im Monogramm, Kreuz und Crucifix*, Schaffhausen 1870

A. Strobel, *Kerygma und Apokalyptik. Ein religionsgeschichtlicher und theologischer Beitrag zur Christusfrage*, Göttingen 1967

V. Tzaferis, 'Jewish Tombs at and near Giv'at ha-Mivtar, Jerusalem', *IEJ* 20, 1970, 18–32

J. Vergote, 'Les principaux modes de supplice chez les anciens et dans les textes chrétiens', *Bulletin de l'Institut Historique Belge de Rome* 20, 1939, 141–63

id., 'Folkswerkzeuge', *RAC* VIII, 1972, 112–41

J. Vogt, 'Crucifixus etiam pro nobis', *Internationale katholische Zeitschrift* 2, 1973, 186–91

id., *Sklaverei und Humanität*, Historia Einzelschriften 8, Wiesbaden ²1972

P. Winter, *On the Trial of Jesus*, SJ 1, ²1974 (rev. and ed. by T. A. Burkill and G. Vermes)

Y. Yadin, 'Epigraphy and Crucifixion', *IEJ* 23, 1973, 18–22

id., 'Pesher Nahum (4Q pNahum) Reconsidered', *IEJ* 21, 1971, 1–12

A. Zestermann, *Die Kreuzigung bei den Alten*, Brussels 1868

INDEX OF ANCIENT AUTHORS

INDEX OF MODERN SCHOLARS